M000073947

A Special Gift

To _____

From _____

High ^{and} Lifted Up

How Seeing Jesus Propelled a Sharecropper's Daughter into Worldwide Evangelism

Jane Lowder

McDougal Publishing is a ministry of The McDougal Foundation, Inc., a Maryland nonprofit corporation dedicated to spreading the Gospel of the Lord Jesus Christ to as many people as possible in the shortest time possible.

Published by:

McDougal Publishing
P.O. Box 3595
Hagerstown, MD 21742-3595
www.mcdougalpublishing.com

ISBN 1-58158-050-9

Printed in the United States of America
For Worldwide Distribution

Dedication

To Rev. Edith Heflin, Rev. Wallace Heflin, Jr., and Rev. Ruth Ward Heflin, who sowed spiritually into my life for more than twenty years.

To the dozens of other men and women who contributed to my spiritual welfare through the years. There are too many to name them individually.

To my mom, who has already gone on to be with the Lord.

Acknowledgments

I must thank Cheryl Wolner, who kept an eye out for sermon tapes on which I had told stories from the past, Rev. Harold McDougal, who put all the pieces of the puzzle together to make the book, Debbie Slayton, who helped me read over the final copy, and everyone else who encouraged me through the years to put the marvel of what God has done in my life into print.

Contents

Introduction

Not long after I gave my life fully to the Lord in 1975, I began to have visions. One of them was a wonderful vision of Jesus on the cross, and when I saw it, I was baptized in the Holy Ghost and empowered for service to the Lord. But that was only one of the many visions God gave me. That particular vision was as real to me the next day and the next as it was in the moment I received it. Like data stored on a computer, I could recall it and relive it at any moment, and I often did so.

Visions, in general, became an important part of how I grew and learned and how God guided me in the days to come. He knew the simplicity of my character and my background, and He gave me this wonderful method of knowing His will for my daily life. Many of the visions I received were very simple, but they spoke volumes to my heart.

Such visions came to me most anywhere and most anytime. For instance, one vision came to me while I was cooking hamburgers in a restaurant I managed not long after I was saved and before I entered the ministry. In the vision, I saw Jesus walking before me, and I saw myself following behind Him. I had a cross on my back. He was looking back at me and saying, "Come on! Come on! Come on!"

Right there in the restaurant I started weeping profusely, and I didn't understand why. One of my co-workers came over to ask me what was wrong, and I told her there was nothing wrong.

"But why are you crying?" she asked, knowing that I usually didn't cry. "What's wrong?"

"There's nothing wrong with me," I insisted.

"Then why are you crying?" she persisted.

"I don't know," I said, and I cried on and on.

I could hardly wait to get off work that night. Shortly after one in the morning, I was able to get away. I got in my car and drove around for the next several hours, sobbing, looking at Jesus, hearing His voice. *If some policeman stops me,* I thought, *he'll think something is really wrong with me, and he'll want to lock me up.* But no one stopped me.

I finally went back to the house where I was staying sometime before five that morning. I parked the car under the huge pine trees in the back yard, but I still didn't get out. The moon was breathtakingly beautiful that night, the sky especially clear. I got down on the floor of the car, and the Lord showed me more of that wonderful vision.

The scene changed, much like turning a page, and suddenly I saw multitudes of people waiting and ready for Jesus, and I saw that He was coming and that He was coming quickly. This thought brought great joy and rejoicing to my heart. I was crying out, "Come, Lord Jesus! Come quickly, Lord Jesus! Come now, Lord Jesus!"

Then the Lord showed me another vision. In it, there was a multitude of people who were not ready for Him. If He came in that moment, they would be lost. My great joy turned to weeping, and I cried out, "Oh, God, don't come until You send me to warn these people!" That vision has never left me and has been one of the strongest motivating forces in my life.

There have been many other visions, and they have enlightened me, warned me, guided me and consoled me through the years and brought me to this present place of leadership in the revival of the end times. I give God all the glory, and I trust that sharing my story with you will bring great blessing to your life. Come with me as we see Jesus *High and Lifted Up.*

Jane Lowder
Ashland, Virginia

But he [Stephen], being full of the Holy Ghost, looked up stedfastly into heaven, and saw the glory of God, and Jesus standing on the right hand of God, and said, Behold, I see the heavens opened, and the Son of man standing on the right hand of God. Acts 7:55-56

The heavens were opened, and I saw visions of God. Ezekiel 1:1

In the year that king Uzziah died I saw also the Lord sitting upon a throne, HIGH AND LIFTED UP, and his train filled the temple. Above it stood the seraphims: each one had six wings; with twain he covered his face, and with twain he covered his feet, and with twain he did fly. And one cried unto another, and said, Holy, holy, holy, is the LORD of hosts: the whole earth is full of his glory. Isaiah 6:1-3

Prologue

Like a Dream

I thought I was awake, but the fact that it all seemed so unreal caused me to wonder. Rev. Ruth Ward Heflin was lying before us in a casket, and people from all over the world, many of them representatives from prominent ministries, had come to pay their last respects to her. The service would be downstreamed over the Internet to people who loved her in every nation.

I listened as the brother in charge of the funeral introduced me, and I couldn't believe what he was saying:

> *Sister Ruth began planning for this day many years ago. As a member of the board of trustees of this ministry, she began telling me more than two years ago about her plans for the future, and she told others as well. She wanted to live, and she had much to live for, but at the same time, she was wisely preparing what has proven*

13

*to be one of the smoothest transitions of leader-
ship I have ever seen among Pentecostal groups.
We Pentecostals have not been known for
smooth transitions of leadership, but Ruth
Ward Heflin has done a praiseworthy job of
preparing us for this day.*

*More than twenty years ago, Ruth Ward Hef-
lin began a ministry in Jerusalem, a ministry
that has grown and prospered through the
years. People now come to the Mount Zion Fellowship from all over the world to be blessed
and to join in the high praises of God that are
conducted there on a daily basis. Through this
ministry, Sister Ruth blessed Jerusalem, and
she blessed all of Israel. She also blessed the
neighboring Arab countries and the entire Middle East. From Mount Zion Fellowship,
Spirit-filled people were sent out to bless the
other nations of the world. This ministry has
made a huge contribution to the present worldwide revival.*

*Many are now asking what will happen with
the Mount Zion Fellowship, and I can say today that it will go on. Years ago, Sister Ruth
set in place leadership in Jerusalem that would
assure its continuance. Sister Nancy Bergen,
who has been with the ministry for the past ten
years, will carry that vision forward. She is of-*

ficially now the pastor of the Mount Zion Fellowship in Jerusalem. I always say of Nancy that the world once had its psalmist David, but now it has Nancy. She also has that wonderful gift of worship that caused King David to bless the world.

During the past several years, Nancy has been in charge of the work in Jerusalem, and Sister Ruth has only visited her occasionally. But the work has gone on successfully, and it will go on successfully. Today, we join together in blessing Sister Nancy Bergen in the name of the Lord. We are fully behind her as she continues the work of the Lord in Jerusalem. From Jerusalem and Zion, may the Word of the Lord go forth to all the nations of the world.

The other element of leadership transition that affects us all here, especially here in America, is the new director of this campground and pastor of the Calvary Pentecostal Tabernacle. She is Sister Jane Lowder, and I want to ask her to come and pray in just a minute as we open this great funeral service.

More than two years ago, Ruth Ward Heflin told me that her chosen successor was to be Jane Lowder. It was a very wise decision, and one that I wholeheartedly applaud. I know that Sister Ruth was happy to choose a woman because she was always eager to see women move into their proper role in leadership, but Jane Lowder was not chosen just because she was a woman. She is highly qualified for the job.

Sister Jane has been with this ministry now for nearly twenty-five years in various capacities. She too has a worldwide vision and has personally ministered in more than sixty-five nations of the world. She is a woman of vision who looks into the heavenlies and brings down the glory of God to the people. Aside from Ruth Heflin, Silvania Machado and Bob Shattles, I have never seen anyone who carries a greater glory in his or her life than the woman who is about to lead us forward into the greater things of God in this new millennium.

For ten years, Jane Lowder led one of the daily services here at the camp. In 1997 and 1998, she became one of the main camp speakers, a privilege reserved for only a few. Due to an auto accident Sister Ruth had in the summer of 1999 and her illness of recent months, Sister Jane has been working closely with Sister Ruth to direct this huge facility and its many outreaches for the past two years. Sister Ruth was totally at peace with this transition of leadership, and those who were in Summer Camp this year know that there was more glory than ever in this place. Yet, Sister Ruth was able to attend the services only infrequently.

Jane Lowder is clearly God's chosen woman for a new millennium. It is my great honor and privilege to introduce her to you today as Ruth Ward Heflin's chosen successor, and I want you to let her know that you are standing behind her and will support her with your prayers and giving. Sister Jane Lowder will now come and lead us in prayer.

Was Rev. McDougal talking about me, Sarah Jane Lowder, the sharecropper's daughter from Stanly County, North Carolina? Were these people standing to honor me? Were these cheers really for me? I was overcome with gratitude to God. How very far He had brought me from those sharecropper's fields.

Part I

Prelude to a Rich, Full Life

One

Days of Promise

I was brought up in an idyllic country setting in rural North Carolina, the oldest girl in a sharecropping farm family of seven children. Dad and Mom were fine, upstanding and hard-working people who believed in teaching us responsibility, honesty, integrity and the dignity of work. All of us worked in the fields together, and because there were no baby-sitters in those days, this training started very early in life.

Before we could do much, we were permitted to ride in the wagon or on the tractor or (my favorite) on the plow. In the early days of our farming, we had two mules — Beck and Jim — and together they pulled the old plow. When we were still quite small, Dad would throw a big rock on top of the plow to make it sink better into the ground, and then he would throw an old sack over the rock and hoist one of us up on top of it. It was a great adventure riding behind the mules as they pulled the plow through the furrows.

21

But it was more than fun. We were learning. We watched how Dad broke up the soil. He would begin with one long furrow right down the center of the field, and then he would work his way down one side and then the other, making sure that every section of the field had been turned over sufficiently so that it would be a good host for the seed. That was a great education in itself.

The old plow was not the most comfortable place to sit, and when it hit a rock or something else hard in the soil, it would buck every which way, and we had to hang on for dear life. By the time the field was plowed, we knew we had had a ride — and we had loved every minute of it.

Learning to ride the plow for hours a day was preparation for greater things to come, for very early in life we were expected to stop watching and start doing the work ourselves. Our duties would not always seem to be nearly as much fun as just riding and watching, but they were each important to our education.

As we worked with our parents from earliest childhood, we learned to imitate them. My highest goal in life was to be able to do what Daddy did and to please him. I loved it when he complimented me on something I had done, and that spurred me on to do more.

But observing and doing were two very different

things. Daddy made everything look easy, but when my turn came to try it, I suddenly discovered that it wasn't as easy as it looked when he did it.

When I was big enough one spring day, Daddy had me walk with him as he drove one of the mules pulling the cultivator. He wanted me to get the feel of it. Then, one day, without warning, he turned to me and said, "Sis, today you can take these lines in your hands, and you can drive old Beck home." I was overjoyed and terribly frightened at the same time. Beck was friendly enough, but she was a huge beast of burden. What a challenge it was for a young girl to drive that mule home!

I had listened to Dad shout "Gee!" and seen the mules responding, and I had heard him say "Haw!" and seen the two mules move the opposite way. He had also pulled the reins, and they were now in my hands. I thought I knew how to do it, but now I had to put my knowledge to the test.

Amazingly, it worked. If I said "Gee!" and pulled on the right rein, the mules moved to the right, and if I said "Haw!" and pulled on the left rein, they moved left. Eventually, this vocabulary became so much a part of my nature that later, when I began to drive a car, I would stick my hand straight out and say "Haw!" when wanting to turn left, or lift it and say "Gee!" when I wanted to turn right.

Then one day, again without warning, Dad said

to me, "Okay, Sis, I'm going to let you try your hand at this cultivator. See if you can take it to the other end of the row and not plow up any of this corn." This was a particular challenge. He hadn't started me off plowing in a field free of plants. That would have been much easier. He had chosen to start me off with cultivating the already growing plants.

I would have to get the cultivator close enough to the rows of tender plants to push up a furrow of dirt against them, but not so close that they would be uprooted and destroyed. Dad wanted me to do this down one side of the corn row and then turn and do it down the other side coming back. Wow! What a challenge!

The plow, or cultivator in this case, had a way of moving the opposite way you pressed on it. If I pressed it to the right, it moved left, and if I pressed it to the left, it moved right. In the process of trying to keep the mule going straight and remembering which way to press the plow, I got so frustrated that I mixed up my "gees" and "haws" and began up-rooting plants and zigzagging all over the field.

It had looked so easy when Dad was doing it, and I thought I had learned, but now I was totally con-fused and not sure what I was doing. Everything I had been taught had taken flight. This wasn't easy at all. I went too far right, then overadjusted and went too far left. When I got to the other side of the field and looked back, it looked like a disaster zone. But I was learning how to use a plow, and I couldn't do it just by watching someone else use it.

That first day, I wanted to give up many times, but Dad wouldn't let me. "Try this other row," he would say. "Keep going." Once in a while, he would coax me with a needed "gee" or a "haw," but he was not about to see me quit. "You'll get it," he said, coming close behind me to be sure I would not be hurt. I was wondering if I ever would learn.

My greatest disappointment was that I had wanted to do the work so well when my turn finally came that Daddy would be very proud of me. I was sure that he must be terribly disappointed. But if he was, he never showed it. He had only praise and encouragement for my work.

I didn't learn to plow well in a day, but I did learn. Before long, I knew my "gees" and "haws" as well as anyone. I could take the cultivator from one side of the field to the other without disturbing the plants. I now knew how to keep that implement in check.

At first, everything about using the plow or culti-vator had been a strain. I strained to move it this way or that and still couldn't get it right. But after a while, it all became second nature. I could just let my hands rest on the plow, and with the slightest movement on my part, it went in the right direction. All I had to do was lean one way or the other, and the plow followed. I became so good at the process that my brother J.C. and I (since we were the two oldest children) became a team and often worked the fields together, while the others planted behind us.

Living and working with five brothers was an education in itself. Talk about women's liberation! I had it long before it became popular. I did everything my brothers did. I dug as many holes as they dug. I cut just as much wood as they cut. I plowed as much ground and picked as much cotton as they did. Living in the Lowder family was as much liberation as I could stand.

After our fields were planted and we had cultivated the crops, there was nothing more that we could do. The plow and the cultivator were idled, and the mules grazed lazily in the fields. Nowadays, with the use of artificial irrigation, much can be done to further the growth of crops. In those days, however, we depended entirely on the Lord to send the rain, and it either came or it didn't come, and we either had a good harvest or we didn't.

Farmers took advantage of those idle times to repair equipment and to work around the barn. Dad made sure we were never idle. The fields, in the meantime, were at the mercy of God.

Then, as harvest time arrived, for one crop after

another, the fields around were again busy with the activity of harvest. When the wheat crop matured, we could see farmers in all the fields around every day checking the progress of their wheat. Little by little, it was changing colors. It became almost white for a time. Then, when the faintest hint of gold began to show on it, excitement spread far and wide. Everyone knew that within days it would be ready to harvest. The changes became very dramatic then, and overnight you could notice a great difference in the color of the grain ... until, one day, it was just right.

Harvesting is so mechanized these days that a few people can do it with their great combines, but in those days, we needed many hands. All the neighbors gathered to help us get up our wheat, and we went to help them when it was their turn to harvest. Some of us cut the wheat, others would come along and tie it into bundles with twine, and still others put it into shocks. When all of the wheat was ready, someone would go and bring the wagon to haul the wheat closer to the granary. We got out the big old threshing machine, and we had a grand threshing party.

These were community events attended by all the neighbors in the area, and all the children came along. For the younger children, it was a time of play, but for the older ones, it was a time of very hard work. No one was excluded. Everyone was caught up in the excitement of harvest.

During that time, when everyone was together, many great stories were told, and we enjoyed ourselves immensely as we harvested and put in the wheat.

If you've never seen a straw stack or had the opportunity of climbing up on top of one and sliding down it, you've missed something wonderful in life. We thought it was the greatest fun in all the world. We would race to see who could reach the top first, and then we would see who could slide down it the fastest and reach the bottom first. What a wonderful time we had! Even Daddy would go up and slide down with us.

Mom and the other women would be in the house preparing the meals and baking pies. It was one of the few times of the year that we had cakes and pies at our home. The only other times were at special holidays like Christmas, Easter and Thanksgiving. Otherwise, we always had jelly for our dessert.

These harvest times were very special, and there was great joy all around. The entire community was happy for us, and we were happy for them. We rejoiced together.

It was a storybook beginning for our lives. But, alas, life was not always to be so kind to us and so much fun.

Two

Days of Despair

Even the joy of harvest was tempered by reality. Not everything we harvested was ours. We had to divide everything evenly with the owners of the land. We carefully measured everything out, and half was paid to them. What was ours could either be eaten or sold to help with other necessities.

For a time, we had a grinder that we used to make our own cornmeal. Later, we took the corn to the mill and had it made into corn flour. We did the same with our wheat. We would go to the mill with wheat and come back with flour. If this idyllic life had continued uninterrupted, perhaps we could have made a go of things financially, but it was not to be.

When Daddy was just forty years old, he suffered a debilitating stroke that left him paralyzed on his right side. He had been working two jobs to keep us in food and clothing. After working all day on the farm, he would get ready and drive the old farm truck (that belonged to the owner of the land) seven or eight miles into Albemarle so that he could work the night shift at the cotton mill to earn extra money for the family. Now he was unable to work at all.

He couldn't walk, he couldn't use his hands, and he couldn't speak clearly. This left him terribly frustrated and concerned for all of us. When we would come into the house, Daddy would start crying, and when he cried, we cried too. It hurt us to see him like that, and we were frustrated because there was nothing we could do to help him. Our future looked rather dim. I was nine years old, and most of my siblings were even younger.

Daddy loved to listen to a certain radio preacher on Sunday afternoons. At the time, the man seemed a little strange to my brothers and me, but Daddy tried never to miss his program. The preacher would tell all those who had a special need in their lives to set a glass of water on the radio while they were listening to his program, and Daddy would have us bring him a glass of water so he could do it.

At the end of the program, the preacher would say, "Now, you drink that water as a point of contact, and God is going to set you free." We thought that was very odd, but in time Daddy's condition did improve. He was eventually able to walk again, to have some limited use of his hands, and to speak. Although he was never able to work a steady job again, his life was much more meaningful. He enjoyed getting back into the fields, if only to supervise our work.

Without Dad's income from the mill, it was very difficult for the family to make ends meet. We children were much too small to work the fields all by ourselves — although we did.

The owner of the farm had kept cows and pigs that we tended. The milk was sold to Carnation. Then the barn burned, and that brought an end to this venture. Our family was eventually forced to go on welfare, and this was our condition for quite a few years.

When I was old enough to work outside the home, I decided that I was going to get a job and help to support the family. I was still studying, but I found a part-time job as a dishwasher in a restaurant called The Barbecue Lodge in Albemarle. I was paid twenty-two cents an hour. J.C. had been working for Roses 5 & 10 (later to become Roses Department Store) two days a week for some time, and now he began full-time work. The two of us went back and forth to town, still helping with the farm chores as much as we could.

When school ended that year, I began working full-time at the restaurant. In order to do that, I had to live in town. I was able to find lodging with the lady who owned the place. Every Saturday, Daddy would come to visit me and get my paycheck.

Later, I went to work in Sanford. The Newton family called to say that they had opened a restaurant near one of the factories there and asked if I would come and help them. I accepted, and worked for them for a while. Eventually, I found that the pay was better at the local shirt factory, so I got a job there. I rented a room from Mrs. Beck at ten dollars a week.

The day I moved in, I carried all of my clothes in a cardboard box. She said to me, "When will you be bringing your belongings?"

I said, "This is it!" That little box represented all that I owned in this world.

Each week I allowed myself only the luxury of buying cigarettes for the bad habit I had developed very young, but aside from that and my ten-dollar room rent, most of my paycheck went to support the family.

I needed a car, and I mentioned to Mrs. Beck one day that I would like to get some extra work on the weekends. She told me about a dairy bar that needed help. It belonged to a friend of hers, and she got me a job there on Saturday and Sunday nights. I saved up enough (a few hundred dollars) to buy my first car from her nephew.

Eventually, I began working other nights at the dairy bar, until I was working seven hours a night from Tuesday through Sunday. I worked both jobs that way for several years, until I eventually became manager of the dairy bar, and I worked there for the next sixteen years.

Daddy kept the family on the farm a while longer after I moved to Sanford, but their lives were very hard. When Mama fell on the steps one day and broke her leg, it seemed to be the last straw. I went home to tend to her while she recovered, and during that time, I rented a little house in the edge of Albemarle and moved the family into it. Our parents lived out the rest of their lives in Albemarle.

Daddy died in 1962, and Mama lived on until 1996. Until the very end, she maintained a wonderful attitude about everything she had suffered in life. She never complained. I never once heard her say, "How are we going to make it?" She was very heroic, and I learned many great lessons from her.

I continued to help the family for quite a while. Aside from my car, my own needs were simple. Mrs. Beck not only gave me the room for ten dollars a week; she also had my laundry done for me and my car cleaned. She had suffered a stroke very similar to my dad's, and she helped me to understand what he was suffering through the years. I deeply appreciated her kindness.

Then, after many years, my life suddenly came to the point of crisis. I became very sick and was diagnosed with emphysema. This was not helped, of course, by the fact that I had acquired a very serious smoking habit. Doctors said that within three years I would have to be on a breathing machine — if I was even alive. I was already taking medicine to help me breathe.

I also had many allergies. I often developed angry welts on different parts of my body, and my windpipe would swell up and make it difficult for me to breathe. Tests determined that I was allergic to thirty-three known substances, and I was forced to take injections three times a week to keep the allergies in check.

At one point, I had suffered from stomach ulcers, and over time the many medications I was taking affected my stomach to such a point that there were many things I could no longer eat. My stomach felt upset a great part of the time.

But my condition was much worse than all of that would indicate. I had suddenly become very despondent. Not a lot of wonderful things were happening in my personal life. I had been occupied with work from the time I had been a teenager, and now, at the age of thirty-four, I didn't have much to show for my years of struggle. With all my work activities, I had somehow forgotten to live, and life suddenly didn't seem to be worth living anymore. Thoughts of suicide assailed me.

This should not have happened. After all, we had

been brought up in Methodist Sunday school and church, and we always went to church on Sundays and never worked the farm on those days. The church we attended was Randle Methodist Church in Stanly County, about five miles from where we lived. Sometimes we walked to church, sometimes the Sunday school superintendent came by to take us, and sometimes we rode in the old farm truck.

Once, during a period of revival at the church when I was twelve, I had a wonderful experience in the Lord. There was much about that night that I never forgot. I never forgot being compelled by the Spirit to go forward because I recognized my need of salvation. I never forgot God changing my life. And I also never forgot the fact that I somehow knew there was now a great call on my life.

But that was as far as it went. I didn't know how to fulfill that call, and there was no one to encourage me, so the call went unanswered for many years. If I had known at the time that the Bible was enough in itself and that I could have found my answer there without someone else's help, perhaps I would have tried. But I didn't know.

I did love the Bible, and I did get to know some portions of it, but I had never learned to seek the Lord and act on His Word. My Bible reading was occasional. For instance, I learned the 23rd Psalm as a child, and I could quote it, but I didn't yet know the meaning of it. I thought it was beautiful, but I didn't know that it was really true. When I heard people say that something in the Bible was not literal and couldn't have happened as it was recorded, it bothered me, but I couldn't prove otherwise.

I did believe that Jesus was Lord. I believed He could do all the miracles spoken of in the Bible. And I even believed that He could do them today — if He wanted to. But I didn't know how to make all that a reality.

I believed in doing good deeds, and I thought I was doing my share. As busy as I was with my work, I still took time to visit the local nursing homes several times a week. I helped to feed the patients I knew, and I stopped to speak to those I didn't know. I took birthday cakes and something to drink with me to the nursing homes and had a little birthday party for anyone celebrating a birthday.

Everybody thought I was a pretty good person, and I thought so myself. Now, however, that all seemed so empty and vain. Inside of me, something was dead, and I didn't know what to do about it. I desperately needed a miracle from God.

Three

Days of Enlightenment

It was at this low point in my life that a friend of mine, Buddy Makepeace, came into the restaurant one day and preached the greatest message I had heard to that point. When he saw how badly I was suffering, he said, "There's hope in Jesus," and he invited me to attend a Full Gospel Business Men's meeting being conducted at the Holiday Inn.

I had known Buddy for years. He was one of us Methodists. He had been a deacon in the church, but his life had also gone through some ups and downs, and when he, too, was at a very low point, God had radically saved him. He told me about it and made me promise I would come to the meeting.

I really didn't want to go to that meeting. I was working long hours, and I wasn't feeling well. And, besides, I was painfully shy and never liked to go to public places where I would have to meet strangers. But I had promised Buddy, and I always tried to keep my promises, so I had to go. There was no way out.

I was forever grateful that I did go. It was that meeting that would be used to turn my life around. It was July 5, 1975.

I berated myself all the way to the meeting for going, but when I walked into the Holiday Inn that night, I was immediately struck by several impressions. One, I noticed how happy everybody there seemed to be. I suppose this was in contrast to how unhappy I myself was feeling at the moment. Second, I noticed that I already knew many of the people who were present. I had met them at church and at work and other places around town. Immediately some of my fears left me.

I sat toward the back part of the room, and soon someone began to lead the group in worship. The singing was nice, but some of the people began lifting up their hands and getting very emotional, and others actually began dancing. This was all very strange to me. We had never lifted up our hands in our church, and we certainly didn't dance in church. I felt very out of place.

Then something VERY strange happened, and it made me wonder if I was in the right place. A lady began speaking in a strange language, and everyone else seemed to be listening to her. But I couldn't understand a single word of what she was saying. I remember clutching at my seat for security and thinking, *What on earth have I gotten myself into?*

Days of Enlightenment

When the woman had finished speaking in that strange language, a lady in another part of the room stood up and began to speak in English. I found her words very comforting and soothing. She said that Jesus was there, that He had come to heal and restore, to lift us up and to put joy in our hearts.

There were many other wonderful parts of the word she gave that night, but when she said that Jesus was there and that He had come to heal, I took hold of it. This is why I was there. I was sure of it. Although I couldn't understand everything that was happening, I was confident of that one fact.

There was a woman to the right of me about three rows up who was suffering some sort of allergic reaction. Her face was covered with big red blotches and welts, and the welts stretched down both of her arms. Suddenly, she began to shake and to cry out, "I'm healed. God's healed me." Although I was again frightened by her shaking and crying, I looked her way just in time to see the welts disappearing from her face and arms.

What is this? I wondered. I was frightened and thrilled at the same time. If this lady could be healed, surely I could too.

A businessman from California was introduced, and he began to sing a special song. In the middle of his song, he would stop and talk a little and then sing some more. Most of his talk was about miracles of healing he had experienced as he laid hands on people around the country. He told of praying for a man who had a hole in his heart, and God had healed him. He told of praying for a man who had been paralyzed from a stroke, and God had healed him. And he continued in this way for a while. They were all wonderful and encouraging testimonies.

After a while, he said, "I'm going to sing one last song. If you are here and you have a broken marriage, God can heal it." As people stood, he sang "Rise and Be Healed in the Name of Jesus." He spoke to mothers and fathers who were not having fellowship with their sons and daughters or with each other and said that God could heal their broken relationships. He assured people that God could do what they could not do and invited them to stand and receive. Then he sang it again.

Then he said, "If you are sick tonight, God will heal you. Stand up and believe Him," and again he sang the song "Rise and Be Healed in the Name of Jesus." Two of us stood, myself and a truck driver. I hadn't intended to stand, but something pulled me to my feet. Before I knew it, I had my hands up in the air. I thought someone behind me had lifted them up, and I turned to scold the person, but there was no one there.

I found this embarrassing, and I wanted to sit

down and to take my hands down, but I couldn't. And I was crying — something I never did.

Peggy Makepeace, Buddy's wife, came over to me and asked if I would like to renew my vows to the Lord. That sounded good to me, and I began to repeat the prayer she led me in. I don't remember a single word of it, but I know that something wonderful happened in my life as I prayed that prayer. An unspeakable joy suddenly filled my soul, and Jesus stepped out from the pages of the Bible and became a living reality for me.

For the first time in my life, I suddenly knew that if I died, I would be with Jesus. I was ready to die or I was ready to live. It no longer mattered. Whatever happened, I wanted to serve the Lord.

That night, the Lord took away all despondency and thoughts of suicide and all desire for death. Now, I had a desire to live, and somehow I felt sure that the Lord would help me with my problems.

When I finally got home that night, I was afraid to go to bed for fear that the joy would not be there the next morning. This was an unfounded fear. The joy I had felt that night would not abandon me in the days to come. This was real.

Four

Days of Healing

After the meeting that night, I felt so good that I
went out with some of the brothers and sisters and
did something I had not done in years. I ate things I
hadn't been able to eat in a very long time, and I felt
no ill effects. Clearly, I was on my way to physical
healing.

Over the coming days, I noticed that some of my
problems persisted, but I felt sure that the Lord was
working on my behalf. I fully expected to receive
His miracle for all of my ailments. I had a new lease
on life, and I was very excited about the future.

Twenty-one days later, the Lord came into my
room at three o'clock one night. His presence was
as a great light. When that light passed over me, I
knew that I had been instantly healed. I had no more
cough, and my lungs were clear. I never again had
to take medication for allergies. The Lord delivered
me from all thirty-three of them. And He put a new

lining in my stomach. My life had suddenly been turned totally upside down. I had met Jesus in a new way spiritually three weeks before, and now I had come to know Him as my Healer.

The remarkable thing in all this is that no one prayed for me that night. No one laid hands on me to minister to me. Jesus, the Great Healer Himself, came into my room and did the needed work.

I suspended all of my medications, and didn't miss them at all. My coughing was gone, my allergies were gone, and my stomach was healed. I had new lungs and a new stomach lining. And I was getting happier by the moment. Surely God had something very good in store for my life.

Five

Days of Empowerment

In the weeks after those wonderful experiences, I began to attend a Spirit-filled church on free evenings so that I could learn and grow. As shy as I was, I suddenly had a burning desire to tell other people about what God had done for me. In fact, the Lord spoke to me very clearly that I *must* tell it. The very thought of doing that publicly terrified me.

Looking back now, I'm not sure what all my fears were. I suppose I was afraid of not saying things correctly and being criticized by others, of sounding foolish, or maybe of not seeming to have anything important to say at all. Whatever the case, my fears held me back in a very real way.

Every time I had a night off and even after work on Sunday night, I would make my way to the church with the intention of testifying. Many times, I was able to get to my feet when opportunity was given for testimonies, and I tried to say something. But each time I found that I just couldn't do it.

No words would come out. I would tremble with fright, and my knees would feel like they were about to buckle, but I couldn't say a word.

Every time this happened, I would stand there and cry for a while, and then I would eventually have to sit back down without being able to express what I wanted to say. It was a terrible experience.

Then I would sit there in my seat crying and feeling defeated. The enemy was telling me that God wasn't really with me and that I could never do anything for Him. What's worse, he kept telling me that because I wasn't sharing with others what the Lord had done for me, I was going to get sick again. Disobedience, he reminded me constantly, brings suffering. This tormenting experience repeated itself over and over again from July through September of that year.

The thought of getting sick again bothered me a lot, and each time I went to church, I repented that I wasn't doing what the Lord had told me to do. Still, I was powerless to do anything different.

One of those nights, after again standing and not being able to speak because no words would come out, I gave myself to weeping a long time after I had gotten home. In fact, I cried myself to sleep that night.

When I got up the next morning, I felt pretty good, as if all that weeping had somehow purified me. Then, while I was in the bathroom combing my hair,

God called me by name. "Sarah Jane," He said. As I was growing up, my family had called me Sarah, but later in life I had been known to all my friends as Jane. Only my father had ever called me Sarah Jane, and when he did, I knew I was in trouble. Now God was calling me by that double name, and that frightened me. I thought maybe Daddy was calling me from the grave.

Then God called me Sarah. "Sarah," He said, "pray."

It had come to me as an audible voice, and I responded out loud: "I don't have time. I've got to get to work."

I crossed the hall to the bedroom to get my keys, and He said it again: "Sarah, pray."

With this command came a sudden sensation in my body. The night I had been healed, I had felt something like electricity going through my body, and I felt that same electricity now. Now I knew it was God, and I immediately got down on my knees at the end of my bed and began to pray. I poured out my heart to the Lord. My prayer was, "I can't do it; You need to do it for me."

Then I began to see a vision of Jesus. He was on the cross, but He wasn't dead. I saw the nails in His hands and feet. I saw the crown of thorns on His head. I saw His face. I looked into His eyes, and they drew me to Him.

In the vision, I walked toward Jesus, drawn by those eyes of love, and was swept up into an intimacy with Him that is impossible to describe. In that moment, locked in His embrace, I began to speak in other tongues. I had done nothing to precipitate it; it just happened.

As I spoke in tongues louder and louder, I kept seeing that vision and experiencing a knowing and an understanding that was new to me. I suddenly knew that if I had been the only person in all the world, Jesus would have given His life just for me. The thought was overwhelming, and it still brings tears to my eyes every time I think about it.

My voice grew louder and louder, and that was contrary to my nature. I sensed that the Lord was placing a new nature within me, a bold nature.

Then Jesus spoke to me from the cross. He said, "Now, I have empowered you. Go and tell everything that I have done for you, and I will go with you with signs and with wonders." (I didn't remember at the time that those words were in the Bible and was pleasantly surprised when I read them later.)

Just as suddenly as it had appeared, the vision went away, but I was left renewed and empowered. It was a new day for me. I thought I had known joy before, but it was nothing compared with the joy that now broke forth in my life.

I was on an irreversible course of service to the Master, and I was loving every moment of it. He had empowered me, and I now knew that I could do what He was asking of me.

I didn't understand all that God was saying the day when He told me, "I have empowered you," but the truth is that I have never stopped speaking out about His love and His goodness to me since that day. In a few minutes' time, He removed from me the paralyzing fear that had prevented me from telling His goodness, and I have been doing it ever since.

That was a great turning point in my life. From that time on, I spoke out, whether I had just the right words or not. I spoke out without thought of what someone would think or say.

In time, I would realize what a terrible lie the devil had been telling me all along: that Jesus was going to remove my healing. He loved me and wanted the very best for my life. He loved me too much to set me free and then turn around and put me back into bondage.

Two other experiences empowered me. First, two nights straight I had a very unusual experience. In the middle of the night, as I sat up on the edge of the bed, God spoke to me. He said, "I will be with you as I was with Isaac, as I was with Jacob, as I was with Abraham, as I was with Moses." I believed

49

what God was saying, and I began to look for His presence in my life.

The other empowering experience was sparked by a sermon preached one Sunday night by the pastor at the church where I was attending. That night he spoke on prophecy, and he made the biblical statement "All may prophesy." This was an unusual statement because there was only one person in the church who ever spoke out a word of prophecy. Still, when the pastor said this, I believed it. Two other ladies who had gone with me that night did too. Afterward, we discussed it and wondered what we should do about it. The next day was my day off, and we decided to pray all night until we received the ability to prophesy.

We prayed together for many hours, and one by one, each of us prophesied. I was the last to do it, but I knew that what I was saying was from God, and I knew that I now had additional power to work for Him.

Six

Days of Deliverance

I was filled with the Spirit and spoke in tongues for the first time on a Friday in September, and I was invited to go to Siler City on a Monday, about ten days later, to give my testimony. But God wanted to change me more before then.

Many of my allergies (and certainly the severity of my emphysema) were caused by my long years of smoking several packs of cigarettes a day. My brothers and I had started smoking when we were kids, and the habit had only grown through the years. I knew it was bad for me, and I had tried to quit many times, but I could never seem to kick the habit. By now, I had stopped trying. I was still smoking the night I renewed my love to the Lord, I was still smoking the day the Lord healed me, and I was still smoking the day He filled me with the Holy Ghost in my house. How could I get rid of this ugly habit?

Early on Saturday morning, just three days before

the meeting in Siler City, a man and woman came to the door of the restaurant and wanted to come in. It was only 5:00 a.m. We didn't open until 6:00, and we never let people in early if we were alone. But he said they were traveling and needed some coffee, and I knew that one of my companions would be there any minute, so I let them in.

They heard me coughing, and when I took the coffee to their table, the man said, "Jesus can deliver you from smoking, and He can heal you of that cough." I looked at the two of them more closely. To my knowledge, I had never seen them before. I didn't know their names, and I didn't think they knew anything about me. Was the Lord trying to tell me something? Was my day of deliverance nearing? Hope rose in my heart.

I went into the office and prayed that God would deliver me from smoking, and while I prayed, I sat at the desk with a cup of coffee in one hand and a cigarette in the other. I stayed there and prayed for about an hour that God would deliver me from the grip of that habit, and I somehow felt that He had done it.

I didn't stop smoking immediately, but I sensed that something was happening. Every time I smoked a cigarette from then on, I would thank the Lord for delivering me, and I noticed that I was smoking less and less.

That Saturday, the Lord spoke to me again in an audible voice while I was flipping hamburgers at work. I remember well that it was 11:20 a.m.

"What are you going to do about those cigarettes?" He asked.

I said, "Lord, when You deliver me, I'll quit."

He said, "What are you going to testify on Monday?"

I said, "Unless You put the words in my mouth, I can't testify."

Again He said, "What are you going to do about those cigarettes?"

In that moment, deliverance came. It was not a decision that I made or the product of my willpower. It was divine intervention.

I no longer had to think about it. I threw all my cigarettes into the trash can, and with them, I also threw the ashtray. I wouldn't be needing it any more. I just knew it. And from that day to this, I have never again desired to smoke a cigarette.

To me, the remarkable thing in all of this was that my healing was not a result of having quit the habit of smoking. Most of us know that if a person stops smoking, he or she will get better. This is a proven medical fact. But my healing came before I was able to quit smoking. God healed me of emphysema, delivered me from allergies and put a new lining in my stomach about a month before I was delivered from smoking.

Why did He do things in that order? I can only imagine that if I had stopped smoking first, many would have considered my healing to be a natural result of my self-discipline. In God's great wisdom, I was healed first and then delivered — so that He could receive all the glory.

Like many former smokers, I have often thought of the money I spent through the years on cigarettes and what I could have done with it. My deliverance from smoking not only blessed my soul and my body, but it also blessed my pocketbook.

Because I was delivered in this way, I have great faith for others to be set free from the addictive habit of smoking. God can do it for any man or woman without the necessity of having to go through nicotine withdrawal.

I experienced no side effects at all, I didn't have to chew gum, and I didn't gain any weight. Many smokers are afraid to quit because they have heard that those who do almost always gain a lot of weight. It wasn't true with me.

Early that next year, I also stopped drinking coffee, and I didn't drink it for the next twenty years. In recent years, I have begun to drink a little coffee to be sociable. When I first quit drinking it, after having been a serious coffee drinker for many years, I suffered no withdrawal symptoms. God is so good, and He was getting me ready for something greater.

Seven

Days of Calling

When I got back to Sanford after testifying in Siler City, I went by the restaurant to see how things were going. It was good that I did because a crowd of ball players had come in, and the staff desperately needed help. There was another reason God had brought me back there that night. The Lord sent a man into the restaurant with a special message for me. He was Dr. William A. Ward of Richmond, Virginia.

Dr. Ward, brother to Rev. Edith Heflin and uncle to Rev. Wallace Heflin and Rev. Ruth Ward Heflin, had been preaching in Sanford, and Pastor and Mrs. Lloyd Ashby had brought him to our place to eat.

I just happened to wait on Dr. Ward's table that night, and when I approached him to ask what he would like to order, he took my hand and said, "Sister, God said to tell you that you're going to travel the nations of the world, and you're going to evangelize for Me."

I was shocked by those words. I did love the Lord, but being a preacher was the last thing I ever imagined myself doing. I had no idea how one might even get started. I did have a desire to do all that God wanted me to do and to say all that He wanted me to say (because He had saved me, healed me, filled me and delivered me), but what this man was saying was far beyond me.

This man has lost his mind, I thought to myself. I spoke to one of my co-workers who was there that night. "You see that man over there? He's crazy. He just told me that I was going to travel the nations of the world and preach the Gospel. I'm not a preacher."

She looked at me for a moment, and then she said, "Well, I think all things are possible with God, and this must be one of those 'all things.' " She couldn't have known how right she was!

Looking back now, it is difficult to define the significance of that moment. I dismissed what Dr. Ward had said as preposterous and impossible, but his words sowed a seed into my heart that was to grow and flourish over the coming weeks, months and years, until the Lord would indeed take me to more than sixty-five nations, carrying the glorious message of the Gospel.

But first, I had some serious training to do. I was about to enter my spiritual boot camp.

Part II

Off to Boot Camp

Eight

A Visit to the Ashland Campground

Over the coming months I met Rev. Wallace Heflin, his mother and other members of the team from Calvary Pentecostal Campground in Ashland, Virginia, as they came into our area for meetings. I enjoyed attending their meetings because they were people of obvious faith who seemed to be getting a lot done for God.

One of the camp ladies, Rev. Viola Weidemann, held a revival in Pastor Ashby's church, and through that meeting many of my friends were stirred to make a visit to the camp. We had heard that they needed help to get the campground ready for the upcoming summer camp season. The idea some of us had was to drive up one morning, help do some work on the camp, and then come back late the same night.

Monday was the only day I could go (I worked all the other days), so I told the Lord that if He wanted me to go He would have to arrange it on a

59

Monday. The next time Pastor Ashby came to the restaurant he told me that they were planning to go to Ashland the following Monday and asked if I would like to go along. I gladly accepted his invitation.

We arrived in Ashland about ten in the morning that Monday, and many of the camp people came out to meet us. I was amazed to see the appearance of the ladies. One lady had a hole in the sleeve of her sweater. Most of them had terrible runs in their hose. Some of their garments didn't match. I didn't think I was staring at them, but Sister Viola said to me, "Yes, it's really us. We're the same ladies who were in the service in Sanford. This is a workday." It almost seemed that she could read my mind and know what I was thinking.

Many wonderful things happened to me that day. For one thing, I was assigned to paint. Not only had I never painted in my life, but I also had been very allergic to paint. Anytime I would get close to fresh paint through the years, my windpipe would begin to close up, and I would begin to wheeze and gasp for breath. This was the first time I had been around paint since my healing, and that part of my miracle was about to be seriously tested. I painted all day long, I got about as much paint on me as I did on the walls, and I had no allergic reaction to the paint at all. I was rejoicing to know that I was indeed healed.

A Visit to the Ashland Campground

When I went into one of the houses to use the rest room that day, a small dog named Dorji came up and grabbed the back of my leg. I remember turning to him and asking, "What do you think you're doing?" I had been extremely allergic to longhaired dogs, but my encounter with Dorji did not adversely affect me at all. I was indeed healed.

That evening, after we had worked all day and then eaten together in the camp dining room, Sister Viola invited us all to her house to bathe and change our clothes before heading home to Sanford. While we were still in the dining hall, someone had offered me some clothes. I looked the clothes over and found that they were all high-collared, long dresses with sleeves to the wrist. I thought to myself, *I'll never wear this.* Now, when we got to Sister Viola's house, she handed me a dress and said, "Put this on after your shower." That dress also didn't look like anything I would want to be caught dead in.

As we took turns showering, everyone else was having fellowship and being ministered to in her living room. As I went though the bathroom door, I saw one of the ladies who had come with us from Sanford falling in the Spirit. I said in my heart to the Lord, "Don't let me be slain in the Spirit here tonight. I want to hear everything that goes on in this house." I was intrigued by this place.

After I had showered and changed, I went back

out to the living room, and I remember seeing a hand coming toward me. But that was the last thing I remembered. Nearly five hours later I got up from the floor, so that we could all go home.

During those hours in the Spirit on the floor, I had wonderful visions. When I got up from there, I knew that I was called to the nations and that I should go back home and quit my job. I was to move to the Ashland camp to prepare myself for ministry.

That night I also saw a vision of the Lord coming on a cloud. He was so beautiful in His white garments, and the cloud was so heavenly. The vision was so real that I thought He was coming right then — at that very moment.

On the way back to Sanford that night, I had that vision all over again. I could never have imagined in that moment that I would still be here on earth nearly twenty-five years later. I was expecting to go with Him at any moment. I did not remember ever reading in the Bible that He would return as He had gone away (on a cloud), but that's how I saw Him that night in vision.

At seven the next morning, I called my boss and told him that I was resigning my position, effective six weeks from that day, and I began to prepare myself to make a major move.

Nine

Getting Camp Ready for Summer
and Getting Me Ready for Camp

To me, there was something very special about
the Ashland camp. I felt God there, I loved the
Heflin family, and I felt that if I could spend more
time in the camp and around these godly people, I
could learn and grow quickly. Then I could surely
come to understand what God wanted me to do and
how to do it. When I learned that they needed more
help preparing the camp for the summer season, I
decided to go a little early and help them. What I
didn't know was that I needed work to prepare me
for camp, and while I was working to prepare the
camp for the summer, God would be working to
prepare me for camp.

Camp life was a shock for me in many ways. I had
been a Methodist all my life and had only recently
been attending an Assembly of God church when
we had no service at our own church. I had never

seen many of the things I was about to experience in the normal daily camp life.

For instance, I had never been in any church where they had an altar call in every service. I had never seen all the members of a church get up and go to the altar at one time. I had never seen an entire church full of people on their knees or lying on their faces before God.

Everyone who was on the campground would go into Richmond at least four times a week for services, Sunday morning and night and Wednesday and Friday nights. At the close of the message, Pastor Edith Heflin would say to us, "This is your time to do business with God. Come and call upon His name. Come and pray. Seek His face. He's going to do something good and wonderful for you." Then all the people would go forward and, together in the altar area, would lift up their voices and cry out to God. This would go on for twenty to forty minutes every time we went to church. If we didn't go to the altar and pray, everyone wondered what was wrong with us. Everybody sought God.

It was in those days that I began to understand the purpose of the altar. In many churches, the altar is just a place for sinners to come and repent, but God intended it to be much more than that. The altar is a place of worship for all of God's people. It is a place of looking into His face and seeing His glory and being changed by it.

In many other ways, camp life was unlike anything I had ever experienced before. This was, of course, reflected in the dress code, but there was much more to it than how we were expected to dress. For instance, no matter how late we had been out the night before in meetings, someone was assigned to knock on our doors early each morning. We ate breakfast together at seven each morning, and then at eight we were all expected to be gathered for morning prayer.

In these daily sessions, everyone prayed at once, and each of us cried out to God in his or her own way. Then, after we had offered our individual prayers for half an hour or so, someone would take charge of the meeting and we would join in prayer for specific needs — Israel, America, the churches associated with the camp, the camp outreaches, the camp leadership, someone traveling in missionary work, and other more specific needs. Our prayer times were always at least an hour long, and often much longer.

One of our most intense prayers in those days was for the upcoming camp season. Toward the end of each morning prayer session, Brother Wallace Heflin would get up and address us for a few minutes. One of the things he always said was,

"They're coming!" He meant the people who would come to Ashland during that camp season, and he wanted us to be ready to minister to them when they arrived.

For those of us who were new to camp (and there were quite a few of us that year), this seemed to be a stretch of faith. The camp facilities were very rustic, and the camp was located in the woods rather far from anything. *Why would many people come here?* we wondered. *And where would they come from?* We would believe what he was saying when we saw it.

Each morning we were encouraged to know the work we were doing on the campground was not just for the benefit of one or two. It would benefit many. Then what needed to be done that particular day was announced. The grounds required a lot of cleaning, and the Tabernacle, the dining hall and the various sleeping facilities had to be readied. Many buildings needed painting, and there was electrical work to be done.

Everyone worked. Young people were assisting the electricians and driving nails and doing whatever else was needed. After all, there was no one else to do the work. We were all encouraged to learn to spackle drywall, to drive nails, to paint or to do whatever else was required at the moment.

Several times a day, the huge camp bell would ring, and we would know it was time to go to the dining hall for a meal. That bell became a big part of our lives.

From very early on, I was assigned to dish duty. Washing dishes was nothing new to me, of course, and I did the work with joy. I was anxious to get on with the work of evangelizing the world, but I didn't mind the cleaning duties. Everyone else cleaned, so why shouldn't I? After each meal, I would wash and dry and put away the dishes, and then I would return to whatever other job had been assigned to me that particular day.

We did not work alone, and I marveled at this. Brother Heflin always came out and worked with us. He was not one to stay in his office all day. If there was work to do, he was right there in the middle of it. The only liberty he gave himself was the right to stop once in a while to tell us all some great faith story about his mom or dad or sister or uncle.

He had many stories from other countries about how God had healed someone, how God had miraculously supplied some need for the ministry or how God had done some other outstanding miracle. He never seemed to run out of these stories, and they all had the same wonderful ending. He would turn to us and say, "And *you* can do that too," "God wants to use *you*," or "*Your* faith can produce a miracle just like that."

And these were not just words. He really meant it. In this way, our faith was constantly being built up, even while we were doing menial tasks around the campground.

Fasting was also a big part of our training. When I arrived at camp, several people there were on forty-day fasts, and everyone seemed to be doing some fasting. This included men, women, boys and girls. To me, a forty-day fast just did not seem possible. *Not eat for forty days?* I couldn't believe that it could even be done, but quite a few were doing it.

I watched the people who were fasting, and I noticed several things. For one, nobody seemed to be dying from fasting. I noticed that even those who were on long fasts still did their assigned work and were in every service. And I noticed that those who were fasting seemed to be very happy. They were always singing, and that really spoke to my heart. I decided that I wanted to fast too.

I wasn't about to undertake a forty-day fast yet. That was beyond anything I could imagine at the time. But I did ask the Lord to give me a seven-day fast, and I felt that He had done it one Sunday morning in the service.

That day at noontime, I was standing in the serving line ready to get my Sunday lunch (always the best meal of the week on camp), and I was saying to the Lord, "I will start my fast tomorrow." But the closer I got to the serving line, the stranger I felt. It was almost as if an invisible wall had gone up between me and the food. It no longer held my interest. When my turn came, I took only a glass of water and quickly stepped aside. That began my first fast, and God did many great things for me.

For instance, one of the ladies hit her thumb with a hammer and practically tore off her thumbnail. She was in terrible pain when she came and asked me to pray for her. While I was praying for her, God took all of the pain out of her thumb. She was rather surprised, and I was very grateful. I knew that God had been hearing my prayers for myself, but now I saw that He was hearing my prayers on behalf of others.

If God was healing people in this way, I had a need of my own. All my life I had suffered with my right hip. Because that hip often popped out of joint and it was very painful to get it back into place, I had grown accustomed to walking with my right leg turned a little to the right. It wasn't comfortable, and it caused my back to ache, but it seemed to be the lesser of two evils.

Before I moved from that spot where God had done the miracle for the thumbnail, I put my hand on my hip, looked up to Heaven, and said, "God, why don't You heal my hip sometime." I hadn't expected an immediate answer, but it came that way. I felt something turning inside my hip socket. My foot became straight, and that hip has never popped out of joint again.

In many other ways, it was a wonderful time for me. The fasting and prayer and the constant tapping into the faith realm caused me to find supernatural power. This was not true just in a spiritual sense. I literally felt God's strength flowing into me so that I was able to do my assigned chores.

I was not a painter, and the constant paint strokes throughout the long days of preparation for summer campmeeting were very tiring for me. At times, I had to rely on the supernatural strength of the Lord to keep my hand moving back and forth, accomplishing the needed work.

That was one of the greatest lessons I was to learn. God's power was not just for miracles. It was for every day and for everything we needed to do that day. It was not just something we talked about in church. It was something we put to use in our daily lives.

Because I had worked in restaurants so long, I knew what it was to handle heavy restaurant china. The camp china was one of the best Syracuse chinas, and it was very heavy. I was amazed now to discover that as I carried stacks of dishes to put them away, they were somehow weightless, like feathers.

I would put one stack away and then go back for another and another, and each time the experience was the same. I sensed that God was showing me something. I wasn't sure at that moment exactly what all it could mean, but I knew that He could make heavy things feel weightless in my hands, I knew that I could pick up things I would otherwise not be able to pick up and could carry them without a sense of their being heavy. And it was all because He was working.

These experiences were just the tip of the iceberg. There were to be many new experiences in the coming days and weeks. They came in a flood upon us nearly every day.

Ten

Major Adjustments

Not every experience at camp was pleasant. There were many adjustments to be made. Two days before camp opened, for example, it was announced that there were not enough rooms to house us *and* those who would be coming to the camp to be blessed. We were asked to vacate the nice rooms we had been staying in, and we were assigned other quarters. I was told that I would be staying in Cabin 16.

I took my clothes out of the room I had been using, put them in my car and went in search of my new quarters. When I found Cabin 16, it was packed full of things that had been stored for the winter, and the door was hanging off of the hinges. *Surely this is not where I am to stay,* I thought. *There must be something better than this.* I didn't have time at the moment to find a better place because I had some other serious responsibilities.

Mother Heflin had given me my assignment for

the summer. I was to be in charge of the dish room for the three meals each day. All of my restaurant training was going to be put to work for the Lord.

Sister Heflin went on to say that God had spoken to her for me to be in charge of the snack bar. Each night, after the final service of the day, we would provide hot dogs, hamburgers, chips and ice cream to be purchased by the people to snack on while they were having fellowship together.

When she said that, I felt like crying. I had loved my work in the restaurant through the years, but I had come to feel recently that God had something much more important for me to do and that He had "delivered" me from restaurant work and taken it out of my heart. That was the very reason I had resigned my job and come to camp. *Why would God put me right back into serving food when I have just resigned from my job to do something more important?* I was thinking. I found that very hard to understand.

But Sister Heflin was our pastor, and I didn't have the courage to tell her what I was feeling, so I meekly accepted my assignment. She told me that once I got settled in my room, I should go to the snack bar and see what I needed to do to get it ready for the summer. The way it sounded, it could be a lot of work, so the room would have to wait for now. I left all my clothes in the car and went in search of the snack bar. I was amazed at what I found.

The "snack bar" turned out to be nothing more than a roofed area surrounded by chicken wire to keep the animals out. It had a dirt floor. At the back of that area was a small concrete block building that had served for some years as the camp kitchen. A newer kitchen and dining room had been built a few years before, and this area was now given over to the snack bar. Getting this area ready for camp was going to be a major undertaking.

The snack bar, too, was packed full of things stored for the winter, and I had to set about finding a place for all of those things before I could even begin cleaning and preparing the place for its intended use. I had only a day or so to accomplish all of this.

There were some rough tables in the roofed area, and we found some old oilcloth tablecloths left over from previous years that we could use to cover them. None of the cloths matched. They were all different colors. But it was the best we could do under the circumstances.

Before we could do that, we somehow had to get rid of the thick dust that covered everything. After we had swept out as much as we could, we washed it all down with a garden hose. Then we began to believe God for some Clorox to disinfect everything.

Money was so tight, and so many things had to be done in preparation for the campmeeting that it was difficult for us to get our petition through to buy a gallon of Clorox. Eventually we were able to buy it, but we had to divide that one gallon of Clorox between housekeeping, the kitchen and the snack bar. At least we had enough to get us ready for the opening day.

And then there was the required camp dress and hairdo. Everyone wore dresses to match. The only problem with the one given to me to wear was that it was at least two sizes too big for me. Nevertheless, I wore it faithfully all summer long.

All of the women were also required to wear their hair up. This would not have been a problem for me a few months earlier because I had had long hair much of my life and had worn it up for my work. But that spring, for some odd reason, I had cut my hair very short. It had grown out a little since then, but barely enough to put a curler in it. I had come to camp with the popular Afro cut of the day. In time, I would adjust to this new requirement, and my hair would return to normal.

I still didn't have a place to sleep.

Eleven

The Air Is Charged

During the days leading up to the campmeeting, we heard wonderful stories about Brother Heflin's sister, Ruth Ward Heflin. She had gone out from the camp as a teenager to China and served several years there before developing a vision for the nations. From that time on, she had ministered in many countries and had been used to reach kings and queens and emperors, as well as the common people in many different places.

Just a few years before, Sister Ruth had moved to Jerusalem with a group of workers from the camp, and from there she continued to reach out to the nations. Now, we were told, she would be coming to Virginia to preach the opening week of campmeeting, and we were very excited to see her. Her plane was due in on Wednesday, and she was scheduled to speak at the Richmond church that night.

I had not even seen a photo of Ruth Ward Heflin,

and I had no idea what she looked like. I was in for a big surprise.

The worship service was prolonged that night as apparently her flight was late. Still she didn't come. At last, Brother Heflin was just about to step up and speak himself when in the door walked one of the most beautiful women I had ever seen. She was very tall, but it was more than that. She walked totally erect and with an air of authority. She carried herself in a way that I had never seen done before. Just one glimpse of her told us that she knew where she was going and what she was doing.

She went directly to the platform without any sign of embarrassment. Her brother said, "We've been waiting for you"; they exchanged a kiss, and she took the microphone and began to sing her now-legendary song, *I Ask for the Nations.* By the time she had finished singing that song, there was not a dry eye in the place. That was my introduction to Ruth Ward Heflin and her ministry.

Sister Ruth also encouraged us to believe that we could all do great things for God. Even though she had just arrived on a long overseas flight, she took time to lay hands on each one of us that night and to pray for us individually. As she did, we felt a touch of the glory that was upon her.

The closer it got to opening day of campmeeting, the more excited we all got. Eventually, we were all saying what Brother Heflin had been saying all along, "They're coming! They're coming!" We were now feeling it in our spirits too. Our hard work was about to be rewarded.

On Friday, we were all about as excited as anyone could be. Everyone was busy, everyone was singing, and everyone was bursting at the seams with excitement.

Many last-minute instructions were given to us. I was told that I should sit on the camp platform, and I was given that special dress so that I could do that. I'm not sure if I appreciated at the time what a privilege it was to sit on the platform. I do know that I will never forget the oversized dress. But I was so overjoyed that the camp leadership had enough confidence in me to have me sit on the platform that I didn't mind the dress. I wore it with pride.

Those of us who were seated on the platform were to set an example in worship and to assist with the offerings or in any other way we were needed. We were also encouraged to be open and sensitive to the Spirit to speak forth prophecies or words of knowledge as they came to us. I was sure that this was one area where I could participate.

Sister Ruth asked us all to be at the Tabernacle at least thirty minutes before eight that night to go over some of the music we would be using. I needed a lot more than thirty minutes' practice, because I couldn't carry a tune, but as it turned out I didn't get there quite on time. I had to finish the dishes.

Then I had to get some clothes out of my car and find a place to shower and change. I was able to do that in one of the ladies' dormitories, and I got back to the Tabernacle as quickly as I possibly could. I found the atmosphere charged with excitement.

When the clock struck 8:00 that night, everyone was in place, ready to begin the service, ready to begin a new summer camp season, and there was something new in the air. God had given us new strength, and we sensed that He was about to do some great things for us. I personally felt God's presence as I had never felt it before.

As I looked out over the camp crowd, I was amazed. Sure enough, people had come from many parts of this country and also from other countries to be with us for the opening days of camp. Brother Heflin had been speaking the truth, and we were glad we had responded to it.

After an opening prayer, everyone came forward in the Tabernacle and the worship began. Before long, everyone was dancing and dust was rising from the dirt floor. I had never seen anything quite like it.

That night, Sister Ruth spoke on God's love for the nations, and by the end of the service, we were all ready to go forth. And camp was just beginning. It was going to be a wonderful summer.

Twelve

The Altar Calls

As the opening service came to a climax, it was both a wonderful and a painful experience for me. Everyone was excited by what we had been hearing God was doing among the nations, and each of us wanted more power to become an effective witness for Him. We sensed that God was about to do what we were asking in the altar service.

I was saddened, however, because Mother Heflin had told me that I would have to leave the night services a little early to open the snack bar and prepare for the people who would come. That thought was very troubling to me. If I couldn't be at the altar services, how could I grow as I longed to do? Wouldn't I miss out on the things that others were receiving?

I had come to camp to receive from God so that I could minister for Him, and I had come to love the altar times. That was when Heaven was opened, and everyone was receiving. Some were having visions or were taken into trances. Some received a burden for a certain nation. Others received other revelations. How could I miss all of that?

I will never forget what happened that particular night. When the altar call was given and people began to pour into the altar area for prayer, it seemed that my heart would be torn from my body. I needed this time. This was the moment I had been waiting for. How could I leave now? But I knew I had to.

I held back for a few minutes, just to see what I was missing, and then I turned and walked toward the snack bar with my helpers (several children). Tears streamed down my face, and my heart felt as if it was being pierced by a sharp object. But God saw my heart, and He spoke to me about what I was feeling and said that He would take away my sadness.

"How can I ask for whatever it is they are all asking for?" I protested. "If I'm not there, how can I receive whatever the altar call is all about?"

"I will give you what I give them," He assured me. "Just ask Me for what they are receiving, and I will not leave you out."

I wasn't sure how that was possible, and I still had some thoughts of staying longer in some of the services. In the end, I always went to my assigned task as I had been instructed, and I can truly say that the deep sadness I felt that night never returned. For the next twenty years, every night of campmeeting (except the nights I myself was preaching) I got up and left the services early, but I never again felt robbed. While I was working in the snack bar, God would give me what He was giving the people at the altar.

Every time an altar call was given, I stayed for just a few minutes to see what God was offering us, and then I went merrily on my way, knowing that I would receive it as I served the people. God never failed me.

After I had closed the snack bar that first night (at 1:00 a.m.), I went in search of a place to call "home" over the coming weeks. In one of the ladies' dormitories, I found a spare mattress and a double sheet. I folded the sheet and slept between the two halves. It was summertime, and I didn't need anything else. I washed that double sheet and used it all that summer, and I kept my clothes in my car.

Those may sound to some like serious sacrifices, but it's amazing what people will do when they're hungry for God.

Thirteen

I Want It

That next day was one of the most wonderful days of my life. At the 11:00 a.m. service, I saw something that, for me, was life-changing.

Mother Heflin taught that morning, as she did most mornings during the summer, and then she prayed for the people. She had a habit of telling people to open up more to God. Sometimes she even shook their arms a little in a symbolic effort to get them to open more. Then, when she felt that they were sufficiently opened to God, she would pray and prophesy over them.

This all seemed very curious to me, and I watched carefully to see what would happen. To my amazement, I saw people changing before my eyes. Their faces lit up as they heard God's promises for them and felt the power coming from Sister Heflin's hands. Several things happened to me that day as a result of this ministry.

For one thing, I knew in that moment that the long

hours we had been putting into the work of the camp were worth it all. Seeing those faces light up made every sacrifice meaningful.

We had been going to church nearly every night, getting home late and sometimes even changing back into our work clothes to put in a few more hours before we slept. Sleep was no more than a few hours each night, and then we would rise the next morning to go at it all over again. For any other purpose, this rigorous schedule might have been too heavy a burden, but to see men and women so changed was absolutely worth it all.

Some of the work we did seemed tedious, and it was certainly tiring, but now I knew that every stroke of the paintbrush and every sweeping motion of the broom, indeed everything that we had done, was all worthwhile.

That day I determined that I wanted exactly what Sister Heflin had. Her tenderness, her gentleness and her faith that God could use each one of those people touched me profoundly, and I was never the same again. I had risen to a new level of faith and a new determination to have the power that could bring such change into the lives of those I ministered to in the future.

Fourteen

Faith! Faith! Faith!

From the first day we had stepped onto the camp-ground, we had had faith drilled into us. The Heflins themselves were simple people of faith, and they knew that if we were to accomplish anything at all, it would be by faith.

The camp itself operated by faith, and as the opening day of the summer camp season had neared, it became obvious to all of us that we needed a lot of faith. I had looked inside the storage areas and the freezers, and I knew what food was available. At the same time, the camp leaders were talking about feeding hundreds of people every day, three times a day — and without any charge. That was a totally new faith concept for me.

"Jesus never fails," we were continually hearing these leaders say, and everyone was expecting to see some great miracles because of it. I was still very young in the Lord, and I sometimes had to wonder if all the people in the camp had all of their senses "intact." This was not just going to be a miracle. It was going to be a GREAT miracle.

Before camp opened, Sister Heflin came by and prayed over the food in the storage areas. She prayed over all those who would be working in the kitchen. She came into the dish room and prayed over those of us who would be working there. She encouraged us all that God would do whatever we needed Him to do, and He did. I may have been the most surprised person of all when our every need was supplied on a daily basis.

Of all the wonderful lessons we learned in those days, simple faith may well have been the most important. Those were faith-building days. Brother Heflin and Mother Heflin were never with us more than twenty minutes without telling us some faith story, and our faith was growing by what we were seeing and experiencing.

It was this faith that would take us out to nations in the future and enable us to do other impossible things.

That summer, after camp was over, we tore down the old snack bar and made room for a much larger and more modern building to take its place. Our faith was being manifested in visible ways.

Fifteen

The Vision of Deng Xiaoping

In the supercharged spiritual atmosphere of the campmeeting, many wonderful things happened. Not only did many people find Christ as their Savior, but many also received the power of the Holy Spirit, many were moved into new realms of worship, many began to operate in the gifts of the Spirit for the first time, and many were called into the ministry. Campmeeting was like a whirlwind that came into people's lives and turned them upside down, and they were never the same again.

It was not uncommon for many people to receive special visions in these meetings, and these were also life-changing. It was that very first summer that I had what has become known as my most famous vision, the vision of China's Deng Xiaoping. Sister Ruth Ward Heflin wrote very eloquently about this vision in her books, and I prefer to tell the story in her words:

High and Lifted Up

That summer during campmeeting, my brother was very excited about the opening door to China. The first night of camp he said, "Ruth has a wonderful opportunity to visit China. Let's all pray for China and for this open door." We all prayed together.

After the service that night Sister Jane Lowder came to me and told me about a vision she had seen. She had been saved just two years before, and she felt a burden for the camp and came to Virginia early that year to help get the grounds ready for the summer activities. She never left, and is today still a vital part of our ministry. At that time, however, having a vision was still a fairly new experience for her.

"When we all prayed for China," she said, "I had a vision. I saw a man who was unusually short for a Chinese man. He had a round face like a happy face. I saw you standing with him in China. Although I don't know what it meant, I also saw a banner that had just one word on it. It said AGAIN! And God told me that I should give you a bolt of material. I don't understand why, but that's what God told me to do."

I wasn't sure why I needed a bolt of material. I probably needed some new clothes, but I didn't think I needed a whole bolt of the same *color. I encouraged Sister Jane, however, to obey the Lord. Whether I understood what He was saying or not was irrelevant.*

We all were busy, and Sister Jane was not able to act on what God had told her. Then, about twelve days later in the service one night, my brother felt the anointing for China again and told everyone how God had opened the door to that country for us and used a diplomat to get us the needed invitation. "I want us all to pray for China," he challenged.

After the service, Sister Jane came to me as before and told me that she had seen the exact same vision again. "This time," she said, "the banner that was over his head was rolled out in welcome to the Bible. I haven't bought that bolt of material yet, but I don't want to go to bed tonight without giving you the money to buy it."

We hadn't known for sure how many yards of cloth were in a bolt, so we had called a local fabric store and asked. "It depends on the weight of the fabric," we were told. "Some bolts have fifteen yards, some twenty and some thirty or more." Sister Jane felt led to give us enough money to buy a large bolt of material.

The next morning, I asked my nephew David to go to the local 7-Eleven and buy me a Washington Post. *Prime Minister Menachem Begin of Israel was in Washington for the first time since winning that country's elections, and I wanted to see what news there might be of his visit.*

My Israeli friend, Eli Mizrachi, director of the Prime Minister's Bureau (equivalent to our chief of staff of the White House), was traveling with the prime minister. He had asked me to call him at Blair House when I got a chance. I was anxious to know what had transpired the evening before during their state dinner at the White House, so I called him now.

While we were talking, David brought in the newspaper and laid it down in front of me. I began to leaf through it absentmindedly as I talked. Suddenly my eyes were drawn to a photo with the caption: LAST NIGHT, A BANNER, 40 YARDS LONG, WENT UP IN TIANANMEN SQUARE STATING THAT DENG XIAOPING HAD MADE A POLITICAL COMEBACK.

I looked for some other article with more details, but there was none. I knew immediately that this was the banner Sister Jane had seen in her two visions. God was about to do something wonderful in China, and He had revealed it to her. You can imagine my excitement!

The Vision of Deng Xiaoping

The China experts in our State Department, officially known as sinologists, were stunned by the return to power of Deng Xiaoping, the man who would hold the reins of power in China for the next twenty years. In fact, experts from many nations, some of whom were perched on the borders of China, watching every political nuance, were stunned by this turn of events, but God knew it and revealed it to us by His Spirit.

The following day, a few more details about Deng Xiaoping and his amazing return to power emerged. They included the facts that he was unusually short for a Chinese man and that he had a round face that looked to many "like a happy face." That face, the one God had shown Jane in her visions, would soon become known to the whole world.

A few weeks later, when an associate and I made our first trip into China, we took with us a bolt of material (forty yards long) and the clipping from the Washington Post. [1]

When God told me to give that bolt of cloth, I couldn't imagine what it would be used for. *Nobody would want a whole bolt of material,* I thought. I was so glad that I was obedient, but what happened next frightened me.

High and Lifted Up

One day Sister Ruth told me on the platform that she would be going to China and was going to carry the bolt of material I had bought and present it to Premier Deng Xiaoping. I was terrified. What if I had been wrong about what I saw? What if she acted on something I had said, on a mere mental picture, and there was nothing to it? She might go into China and never come back!

I went into a room behind the platform, flung myself on the floor and cried out to God. "Oh, God, put a lock on my mouth. Don't let me say anything that is not of You. Don't let any pictures come into my mind that are not of You."

As I prayed in this way, another vision appeared before me. I saw the closed door of China, but now there was a red carpet extending out from it. Then I saw a baby in embryonic form inside the door. The baby had a key and was opening the door.

On the other side of the door, I saw Deng Xiaoping and Sister Ruth walking together. She had the Bible in her hand, and she was saying, "But you don't know my God." I knew then that the door to China would surely open again and that it would open from within. Many wonderful visions were given to me that summer.

---

1. From *Harvest Glory* by Ruth Ward Heflin, McDougal Publishing (Hagerstown, Maryland: 1999).

Sixteen

A Major Move

The summer came to an end, the last song was sung and the last sermon preached, and everyone went home. Now what?

I knew God had told me to quit my job, and I knew from the beginning that my stay in Ashland was intended for more than the summer camp season, but I had been afraid to tell the Heflins that. I had only asked their permission to stay for the summer camp-meeting season. Now, I trembled at the thought of asking them if I could stay on permanently, but I knew that was what God wanted me to do.

When I told Mother Heflin that I wanted to quit my job permanently and move to the camp, she cautioned me: "Now, don't go home and give all your stuff away, because you might not like the way we live. You might not like the way we dress. Many people don't, and they don't stay long."

I wasn't afraid of any of those things. I already had a taste of camp life, and although there were many personal sacrifices involved, I didn't mind that. I had one pressing thing on my mind. I had watched Mother Heflin minister throughout that summer, and I had seen people's lives changed because of the love and power of God that was in her. I wanted that. If it meant wearing a long dress and putting up my hair, I didn't mind.

There was something about her that was so radiant and yet so gentle, and so outreaching to others, that I was determined to have it. She welcomed me with open arms, and I never looked back.

What she had told me was good, sound advice, but I was not about to run from what God was handing me on a platter. I was going to have His very best for my life.

It didn't take me long to move the remainder of my things, such as they were, to camp, and Ashland, Virginia, became my permanent home. It has remained my home ever since.

Seventeen

My Continued Formation

After the summer campmeeting had ended, the camp became a very different place. Now we had to get back to our day-to-day business. Our activities that fall were to set a pattern for years to come.

The very next day after the camp activities came to a close, we began tearing down the old snack bar to erect in its place the new building. Very often, during camptime, the Lord would speak of growth, and the next months would be occupied making room for that growth.

Another important activity occupied a major portion of our time. Each year, classes would be conducted for those who wanted to learn the basic Bible teachings. That year there was a six-week course that we were all required to attend. Along with the basic Bible teachings, we were taught to have a vision for the nations, and we were all believing to be able to accompany Brother Heflin on some of his upcoming trips overseas. I made my first trip to Israel that same fall.

So a portion of our day was spent in prayer, another portion in study and another portion in work on the grounds, and we usually went to church somewhere at night. With all of this, we did manage to get a little sleep, but never more than the bare necessity. There was too much to be done. We had a very intense schedule, as the boot camp environment that I had discovered when I first came to the camp continued. Our life was, in many ways, comparable to military life.

I did my first forty-day fast that fall, and from then on I would do at least one and sometimes two a year. None of us died from fasting, and we all grew immeasurably in the Lord.

A twelve-foot-deep hole was dug for a basement for the new building, and the next spring, when the winter thaw and the spring rains came, we were often needed to work down in that hole cleaning it out and getting it ready for the blocks to be laid. I was hauling heavy buckets of mud out of that hole as I fasted.

On the thirty-seventh day of my fast, a truckload of concrete blocks arrived about noon and had to be unloaded. The problem was that they needed to be lowered down into that twelve-foot-deep excavation. Most of the available helpers were women.

We were able to devise a sort of chute, and a couple of men unloaded the blocks and sent them down the chute to us. We women got in a line and handed each block from one lady to the next until they reached the pile in the center. There, two men stacked the blocks. We eventually got all the blocks down into the basement, but in the process each of us had to handle all five hundred of them.

It was time for lunch, and as soon as all the blocks were unloaded, the others left for the dining hall. Suddenly I found myself alone. I was feeling very weak from the long fast and the exertion of passing the heavy blocks, and it suddenly dawned on me that unless the Lord helped me, I wouldn't be able to get out of that hole by myself. I didn't think I could get up the ladder.

I was able to pull my weight up to the first rung of the ladder and the second, but then I was too exhausted to go on. I laid my head on the next rung and said, "God, what am I going to do? How am I going to get out of here?"

He said to me, "Sing Me a song."

I didn't think I could even sing. But I had to try, and I was surprised at what came out of my mouth. From my spirit I was singing "The Joy of the Lord Is My Strength." As I sang, I gained strength, until I was able to get up the ladder and out of the hole.

It was still early in the day, and I wondered how I

would get through the rest of it. I would certainly have to do a lot of singing. I went into the closest rest room, washed my face and hands, and went into the dining hall to get a hot cup of tea.

After I had sipped that tea and sat for a little while, I felt my strength returning. I was able to go back to work, and I worked until eight or nine that night. I tapped into something important that day that has been with me ever since. I know where to get my strength. I know where to go when I lack it, and I am able not only to utilize this supernatural strength for myself, but also to bless others.

I had so many lessons to learn. Some of them came easily, and others cost me something.

After camp that previous fall, I had been assigned to live in a building we called "Green Doors." Eventually, three other women were assigned to share my room. Space was very limited. I had a top bunk, and it was difficult to get out of bed without getting my foot in the mouth of the lady sleeping in the lower bunk.

Green Doors often experienced dampness, and patches of mildew were constantly appearing. This mildew tested me in a very different way, one that also changed my life.

Aside from a limited space to hang our clothes and small drawers for our personal items, the only storage space in those rooms was under the bed and on one small rack attached to the wall. It held a single suitcase. Since I was the first lady assigned to that room, I had put my suitcase up on the rack. Then I went away for a few days, and when I came back, I noticed that my suitcase was no longer on the rack. One of the other ladies had moved it and put her own there in place of mine.

I didn't say anything at the time, but as the weather warmed up, I began to need some of the clothes I had stored in that suitcase. One day I opened the suitcase to get something to put on, and I found that the article of clothing I was looking for was green with mildew inside and out. Alarmed, I took out more clothes and looked at them. They were all the same.

Most of the clothes I had in that suitcase were brand new, and many of them had never had the original tags removed. I had bought them while I was still working and had never yet worn them. I was very upset now to see how musty they had all become.

I put everything back into the suitcase, slammed it shut and went out the door with the suitcase in my hand. I was going to find some of the leaders of the camp and complain.

I had always walked fast, but now I was walking particularly fast. I was angry, and I wanted everyone to know it. I was ready to give someone a piece of my mind.

The first leader I saw coming across the campground was Sister Viola Weidemann. I rushed up to her, opened my suitcase and threw it on the ground. In the process, I purposely dumped all of my clothes out in front of her on the ground, and I said disgustedly, "Just look at this!"

She looked at me very calmly and said, "What does that have to do with the coming of the Lord?" And she walked on calmly toward her destination.

I stood there dumbfounded for a moment, not knowing what to say or do. I thought over what she had said. What *did* this have to do with anything important?

Suddenly, I realized that I had a choice to make. I could insist on making a big deal of this little problem of some damp clothes, or I could get on with my pursuit of God and His will for my life. My choice that day set a pattern for my life in years to come. I picked up the suitcase and put the clothes back into it, and I set off for the prayer chapel to pray and seek God. Inside, I asked Him to forgive me for my lousy attitude, and I asked Him to put His love and grace within me.

From that day forward, I was never bothered by clothes. My clothes could be green with mildew, some garment could suddenly have a hole in it that I hadn't noticed before, or something I had particularly loved to wear could suddenly be unfit to wear

again. But none of this ever bothered me again.
These were petty things. In the prayer room that day
God delivered me from caring about the insignifi-
cant. If something didn't pertain to the coming of
the Lord, it didn't "mean a hill of beans" to me, as
we country people are prone to say.

As we acquired the godly habits of prayer and fasting, of obedience to the voice of God, of being on
time for and joyously participating in all activities,
of having our own times of devotions with the Lord,
of giving sacrificially and prophetically to the Lord's
work, we matured and got ready for our future ministry to the nations.

Part III

To the Nations

Eighteen

Around the World With Wallace Heflin

The frequent tours that Brother Heflin often led to Israel and to other countries helped many people get started in missions, and I was among those who benefited. As I said, I went with him first in the fall of 1977. It was a very moving experience to walk with many other believers in the Bible lands. We toured the holy places in Israel and Jordan, and we held many wonderful worship services as well as evangelistic meetings at night. This was our introduction to other lands and other peoples, and it developed in us a great passion for the souls of men and women everywhere.

My next missions trip, early that next year, was with two other ladies — Viola Weidemann and Pattie Chappell. Sister Ruth flew in for just one night's service, and when she did, she prophesied over the three of us that many open doors awaited us in Australia. We left in February for about a month of meetings, and it was my privilege to use the savings I had left from my working days to pay for the trip.

During the time we were in Australia, God opened many wonderful doors to us, especially among the Aborigines, the natives of that country. The other two ladies did the preaching, and I lent them my support through testifying and helping to minister to the people in each place. We prayed for people in churches, in their homes and in other public places where we met them. Those early trips with other missionaries were days of much learning and growing for me.

After camp that summer, Brother Heflin decided to take a group of us around the world for meetings in many countries. We first did the Holy Land tour with a larger group. When that was finished, most of the tour members flew back to America, but nine of us continued on — bound for Iran, India, Nepal, Indonesia and Australia.

I was still relatively new to these things, and the trip presented many challenges. One of them came in Ahmedabad, India, with Pastor Joshua Raj. By the time we arrived there, it was already November. Brother Heflin wrote about this experience in his book *Power in Your Hand:* [1]

In November of 1978, we were late in arriving for our scheduled meetings in Ahmedabad, India, because we got stranded in the turmoil of the deteriorating situation in Teheran, Iran. We finally arrived in India on what should have been the last night of the meeting. There were about two hundred people present. I preached that night. Afterward, I did not feel that the meeting should close, although many of us were scheduled to go on to other places. I asked some of the others who were with us if they would be willing to stay and continue the meeting.

The first person I asked answered, "No."

One young brother from the Midwest said, "My wife and I would like to stay."

A young sister from North Carolina [that's me] *said, "Brother Heflin, I'd like to stay too." So those three stayed on in Ahmedabad to continue the meeting.*

The three of them were young in the Lord and together didn't have great things to offer, but "SUCH AS [THEY HAD]" they were ready to give. No mission board would have sent them out, but "SUCH AS [THEY HAD]" they were willing to impart to others.

We were gone for three or four days. When we came back, the meeting had grown from a couple of hundred to nearly a thousand. I went out for three or four more days, and by the time I got back, there were nearly two thousand, five hundred people attending the meeting.

What had happened? That young brother started giving out what he had, and the Holy Ghost started multiplying it. His wife started giving out what she had, and the Lord started multiplying it. That "Tarheel" [that's me again] *started giving out what she had, and the Lord multiplied it.*

A man had been hit by a car. His legs and arms were broken. They prayed for him one afternoon. God healed him, and the crowd automatically doubled. The place was shaken by the power of God. When I got back there, I saw that they had roped off the front of the meeting area, and I asked why.

"Brother Heflin," they told me, "you will never believe it. We had a fist fight last night in church."

I said, "You had what? In church?"

"The people wanted to get prayed for so badly because miracles were taking place that they began fighting over who was going to be first in line."

"What did you do?" I asked.

"We got the biggest Indian we could find and put him over the healing line."

Why did it happen? They were giving "SUCH AS [THEY HAD]" and the Holy Ghost used it. It grew and grew and grew and grew some more, until it was sufficient to meet the need of the hour. And that which is in you will grow in the same way. We are going to give "SUCH AS [WE] HAVE" to the lost and dying world, and Jesus will come and put His hand of multiplication upon it. God will do the work.

God had done such great miracles through Brother Heflin that it was hard for us to follow him. But the people were hungry for more, and we were willing to do what we could. Rich Shope was a young minister, and he did the preaching during those days. I supported him as I had been doing for others. We were all amazed by what God did.

When it was time for the team to move on to Nepal, several of the ladies felt led to stay in India and minister in the villages, and I was led to remain in Ahmedabad to work with Pastor Raj. He had asked for a volunteer to stay behind, and I had responded. The team members would all meet again in Bombay eight or ten days later and continue the journey together around the world.

The reality of what I was volunteering for didn't hit me until I was standing at the airport watching the rest of the team fly off. Pastor Raj turned to me and said, "There's a man here who wants you to pray for him." I didn't have a problem praying for the man, but I was sure that he was expecting more than prayer. Brother Heflin and others in the team had been prophesying personally over many people in the meetings, and this man was expecting me to give him a word of prophecy. I had conquered my fears long before of giving a public prophecy for an entire congregation, but giving personal prophecy was still a very scary prospect for me.

What if I told someone the wrong thing and he or she acted on it? Everyone else had now gone, and I was suddenly feeling very much alone.

We went into a side room, and I began to pray over the man who wanted prayer, and as I prayed, God gave me a word for him. This sparked a chain reaction, and one by one, they brought to me all the personnel in the airport, and I ministered to them all in prophecy. Some of them were saved that day, and others were healed. It was a wonderful break-through for my ministry.

I was feeling very good about the ministry we were going to have in Ahmedabad ... until we arrived back at the pastor's house and I saw a hundred and fifty people gathered in his yard. I was shocked and wondered what would be expected of me.

I asked Dr. Raj, "What are all these people doing here?"

He said, "They're waiting for *you*."

A big lump suddenly formed in my throat. I was alone, and I had no idea what I should do next.

"Let me go into the house," I said. "I'll be back in a minute." I went up to the room where I was staying and shut the door. Once inside, I lifted up my hands to the Lord and said, "Oh, God, help me!"

I grabbed my Bible and went back outside. On the way, I opened the Bible, and I read from the place it opened to. I didn't know how else to do it. I had spoken once or twice at camp, I had given testimonies in many places, and I had gone to Raleigh, North Carolina, for a three-day meeting, but otherwise I had never preached and didn't really know how.

I don't remember what I read that day from the Bible, and I have no idea what I said to those people. What I do remember is that when I opened my eyes, I saw that scattered individuals throughout the crowd were weeping. I did an altar call, and about twenty-five people came forward and gave their hearts to Jesus. Many were filled with the Holy Ghost. There was a blind boy there, and God opened his eyes.

After I finally finished ministering to the people, I went into the room and fell on my face with thanksgiving for what the Lord had done. How gracious of Him to save me from disaster and to give me such victories.

A little later, however, Pastor Raj came to the room and said, "There's another meeting tonight at eight o'clock at the Methodist church," and I was instantly thrown back into turmoil. *Oh, no,* I thought. *Preaching and praying for people in someone's yard is one thing, but now in a church and a formal one at that.* My fears, of course, were unfounded. God did the same things that night in the church that He had done in the pastor's yard.

Those first two meetings established a sort of pattern for my ministry for the years to come. I would read a portion of scripture and do what I knew to do, but there would invariably come a moment when I didn't know what to do next. As I sought the Lord in those moments, He would reveal to me things about the people who were there in front of me. This would come either through visions or through words of knowledge. As I would begin to call out the things the Lord was showing me, people would be saved and healed and filled.

I had often seen Brother Heflin use a three-step approach to ministry in places like this where many people were new to the Gospel. He would first call for those who wanted to be saved. Next he would call for those who wanted to be filled with the Spirit. And, finally, when those two groups had been ministered to, he would pray for the sick. I used that approach sometimes, and it also yielded good results, but more often than not, God just did it by His Spirit.

For instance, in that second meeting in India, as I was calling for those who wanted to be filled with the Spirit, the presence and power of God was suddenly felt in that place, and the people began to receive the baptism of the Holy Spirit right where they were sitting. It was awesome. I couldn't say anything. I just watched. God didn't really need me, and He was letting me know that fact. He was giving me the privilege of being used to minister to those people, but He could have easily done it without my help.

Before long, people began to get up and come to the front and declare their healings. One lady had been paralyzed for more than thirty years, and God healed her that night. Another lady couldn't walk, but God healed her. Many other wonderful miracles happened as the power of God flooded the place. And I had never even prayed for the people. It was all done by the sovereign power of God.

In the midst of all that, the Lord spoke to me and said, "I will never leave you nor forsake you. And I will always confirm My Word with signs and wonders if you will go for Me." In that moment, I knew that I could go anywhere and face any type of situation, and God would move and honor His Word. That experience changed my life.

Another amazing thing happened that day. I suddenly realized that I would never be homesick, no matter where I was. I could feel at home in any nation on the face of the earth, and I can say that after visiting more than sixty-five countries, I never felt homesick. It would have been just fine with me if I had never come back to America again. I was at home wherever God wanted to take me. What a gift that proved to be!

There were many other highlights of that wonderful trip. It was a long and rewarding one. Toward the end of the trip, when we should have been nearing home, it was decided that we should go into Quito, Ecuador, to strengthen the McDougals and their team working there in that Andean capital.

When we arrived in Ecuador, I was feeling especially low for some reason. We had been going hard and long for many months, and perhaps I was just especially tired. One night, I was feeling very discouraged. We had gotten up early that morning and spent much of the day preaching in the Indian markets. Many had responded favorably to our message, but others had thrown tomatoes at us. My face had gotten blistered from the intense sun there at the equator.

There must have been more to it than this. Looking back, I wonder if I was not feeling the weight of the important spiritual decisions being made in that city. Whatever the case, I suddenly felt like the weight of the world had dropped onto my shoulders. It seemed to me that others were so much more talented than I was and so much more spiritual, and I wondered why God really needed me in His Kingdom at all. Was there a place for someone like me? I wasn't feeling very useful at the moment.

I was standing at the sink washing dishes in the large, unfinished house outside the city that a kind brother had loaned to the Quito team. *At least I'm good for washing dishes*, I was thinking to myself. In that moment, Sister Diane McDougal came up behind me and said, "You have the makings of an excellent missionary." She could not have known how encouraging those words were to me at that moment. I never forgot them. God did have a place for me in His great harvest fields. He had shown me that fact in India, and I could not afford to let that knowledge slip from my spirit in the days ahead.

1. Heflin, Wallace H., Jr., *Power in Your Hand*, McDougal Publishing (Hagerstown, Maryland: 1998).

Nineteen

Egypt, My First Love

That summer I received prophecies from several different people, and they all said more or less the same thing. The Lord wanted to send me out to the nations, and I would be going alone. I knew what at least one of those "nations" would be. Several years earlier, even before I had gone to the camp to live, God had given me a wonderful vision of Cairo. It was an extremely simple vision. I saw the name Cairo in neon lights. I didn't even know where Cairo was or even that it was a place, but when I called Pastor Ashby in Sanford and described the vision to him, he told me that Cairo was the capital of Egypt. From that moment on, I carried a great love in my heart for Egypt and the Egyptian people and had been praying and believing that I would one day go there.

When I had that vision, God told me that Cairo would be His gift to my heart, a precious jewel that

I would treasure. She would be more precious to me than any diamond. Now, apparently, my time had come to visit her.

When I spoke of this with some of my camp companions, several of them warned me that it was against normal camp policy for someone to travel alone. It just wasn't done. "Neither Mother Heflin nor Brother Heflin will let you take a trip alone," I was assured. Still, I could not get it out of my heart how clearly the Lord had said, time and again through the summer, that I was to do just that.

The thought of approaching either Mother Heflin or her son, or both, and explaining what I wanted to do frightened me terribly. Finally, I got up my nerve one day and asked if I could go into Brother Heflin's office to speak with him. He was a big man, and when I came into his office that day and saw him sitting behind his desk, he seemed to loom even larger. I sat down in a chair facing his desk, and I seemed to shrink in size before him.

When I tried to speak my lips trembled, and I had difficulty forming the words. I just sat there for a moment, trying to pull myself together.

For a time, he just looked at me, waiting for me to speak, and when I didn't, he said, "Yes, Sister Jane? Did you want to say something?"

With that, I just blurted out the whole thing, the vision and the prophecies. Expecting him to say no,

I had typed up all the prophecies I had received and was ready to present them to him word-for-word so that he could see what God was saying to me.

I was on the defensive, as I told him, "When you preach, you tell us that we must be obedient to what the Lord is speaking to us. Others in the camp leadership preach the same thing. But now everyone is telling me that you're not going to let me go and do what He is telling me to do."

He had a big smile on his face as I handed him the typed version of the prophecies. He sat for a while, calmly reading over each of them. Then, when he was finished, he said, "Do you believe that God is calling you to go?"

I said, "Yes, sir, I do."

He said, "Do you believe He's telling you to go by yourself?"

I said, "Yes, sir."

"Well," he said, "I know a pastor in Cairo. I haven't seen him for a while, and I can't say for sure that he hasn't moved or that his phone number hasn't changed, but I'll find the number I have and we'll call and see what we can find out."

As I left his office that day, it was with mixed feelings. In one sense, I was floating on air because of the thought of being able to go to Egypt, but in another sense, I was very frightened at the prospect. Did I really want to travel to Egypt alone? I wasn't so sure now. But God had said it, so I had to do it.

In the end, we were unable to reach that pastor by phone before it came time for me to leave, but Brother Heflin made sure that I had the phone number with me, and he also told me about a hotel he had stayed in once when he was in Egypt. He told me how to get a taxi at the airport and where to go. From the hotel, I would try to locate Pastor Sammy Labbib. If I couldn't locate him, I was on my own.

"Just as God has told you to go," Brother Heflin assured me, "He will tell you exactly what to do. If the pastor is there, he will help you. If not, the Lord will have someone else." In this unusual way, I made my first trip alone outside of my country.

When I arrived in Egypt, it took quite a bit of time to clear customs and immigration, and by the time I found the hotel and got settled, it was already too late to start calling. I went to bed, intending to find Pastor Labbib the next day.

I woke up early the next morning and began my search for the pastor. I quickly learned that Egypt was not like the United States, and finding someone was not nearly as simple. Amazingly, after a while, I was able to locate the pastor. I began to tell him who I was and why I had come. I managed only to say my name, where I was from, that God had told me to come to Egypt and that Rev. Wallace

Heflin had given me his name, when suddenly the telephone line went dead. It remained dead for the next eight hours.

I had booked just one night in the hotel, and I didn't want to spend any more money, so I checked out and sat in the hotel lobby praying. If God had sent me to Egypt, surely He would help me to know what to do next.

Every few minutes, I went to the telephone and tried to call Pastor Labbib again. Late that afternoon, I finally got through.

After the line had gone dead that morning, the pastor had sat by his phone for hours waiting for me to call back. When he couldn't wait any longer, he had his daughter Ruth wait for the call. It was Ruth who answered when I finally got through. She told me that her father wanted to welcome me into their home, and she gave me the address. I could get a taxi going there, she said.

As I looked for a taxi to take me to Pastor Labbib's house, I rejoiced in the wonderful release I felt in the Spirit. Someone was offering me a place to stay. Although I had never met this family and they knew nothing about me, they were willing to help me. What a miracle! This had to be God.

Cairo is a huge city, and the traffic there was the worst I had ever seen in my life. As we inched along in the afternoon traffic, all sorts of thoughts went through my mind. The hotel manager had written down the directions given by Ruth and had handed them to the taxi driver, and he had even given me a copy in English. But still I had no way of knowing if we were even moving in the right direction. Was it safe for a young American woman to be alone in such a large and strange city?

What's worse, I was not the only one in the taxi. There were three Egyptian men in the cab with me, and I could tell they had been drinking. I had no idea what they were saying, but one thing I knew. God was with me, and that truth forced aside every other thought. Everything was going to be okay.

We finally arrived at the pastor's house beside the church, and he had people watching for us. I was welcomed graciously.

It was very interesting to me that not long after I arrived at the Labbib home, someone from the hotel called to see if I had arrived safely. The thoughtfulness of this overwhelmed me. Later, I learned that foreigners were tracked from place to place in Egypt (as they are in many countries). I had a lot to learn. Each time I left Pastor Labbib's house in the days ahead and went to stay for any length of time somewhere else, my movements would have to be reported.

My first meeting in Egypt was a house gathering with some fifteen or twenty people. As the service progressed, I didn't understand anything that was being said or done. When it was my turn to speak, I had an interpreter, but until then, I was on my own. I soon learned the secret of what to do in these situations, and this was to serve me well throughout the years. As the Egyptian people sang in Arabic, I sang in English and in other tongues. If I hadn't done that, I would have just been there doing nothing while they worshiped, and that would have been terrible. I needed to worship just as much as they did. I sang too, and when my time came to minister, I was ready.

As the people had been coming in, I was pondering what I should say or do, and the Lord drew my attention to a picture of Jesus on the wall. The Lord said to me, "I need to come down from the wall and into their lives. I need to give them My heart." When my turn came, I began my sermon with that picture of Jesus on the wall. He was happy that we had a picture of Him, I told them, but He wanted us to have much more. He wanted us to have *Him* living in our hearts.

Three people came forward and expressed a desire to know Jesus as their Savior that day, and as I prayed for the sick, God did seven wonderful miracles. I remember that one was the healing of a back and one the healing of an infected ear. A little girl who had been unable to walk was brought by

her father. "If you think your Jesus can do something for her," he said, "please pray for her." I
prayed for her, and God healed her.

The man began weeping. After a while, he pulled
up his shirt and said, "Do you think God could do
anything for this?" He had very long scars from an
operation, and they were not healing properly. The
surgery had been performed months before, but in-
fection had set in and the scars would not heal.

I said to him, "No, I don't *think* my God can do it.
I *know* my God can do it." And God touched him
and healed him. He was also saved, and his whole
family was saved because of that miracle. God was
helping me.

Quite a few of those who had come received the
baptism of the Holy Spirit. All in all, it was a wonderful, faith-building experience.

In the coming days, Pastor Labbib became like a
father to me. He opened doors of ministry for me
around Cairo, Ismailia, Alexandria and many other
cities and towns of Egypt (some of them with names
that I couldn't even pronounce). God did many great
miracles in each of those places. I had officially begun my ministry among the nations.

Twenty

The Golden Door

I went back to Egypt several times after that, and because I loved the country so much, I became determined to go there and spend the rest of my life.

On one particular visit, I had been in Egypt for about six weeks and was kept busy in wonderful meetings during all that time, but I was due to visit Sister Ruth and the rest of the Mount Zion Fellowship team in Jerusalem for Christmas. Once there, I planned to stay a couple of months with them in the Holy City before returning home.

On my way to the airport in Cairo that day, God gave me a vision. I saw what appeared to be a large iron or brass door. It seemed to be the gate to some city, and it was swinging shut. There was a large pin that could be slid closed to prevent the door from opening, and it was not closed, so the door could be opened. But, for the moment, it was closed.

There was more to the vision. As the one door closed, I saw another door open. This door was golden. Suddenly, and for seemingly no reason, I had the feeling that my great love for Egypt was slipping away from me. My great desire toward her was dissipating, until it almost felt as if it had never existed in the first place.

This all seemed very strange to me because while I was having this vision, Pastor Labbib, who had been so kind to help me arrange much of my ministry in Egypt, was right there with me in the taxi. He was very graciously accompanying me to the airport.

I was troubled by what this vision could mean and about what I was feeling, but I didn't have time to deal with it at that moment — and I didn't know how. I would believe the Lord to give me more understanding of what He was saying while I was in Jerusalem.

When I arrived in Jerusalem, I felt the intense excitement of being in the Holy City, but the vision I had received in Cairo on the way to the airport was strong in my mind.

We met each morning for prayer from eight until twelve noon. There was a very wonderful, spiritually charged atmosphere in those meetings, and I felt privileged to be there, but still I somehow felt miserable. I was feeling guilty because I wasn't praying for Egypt as I had been praying for her now for the past several years. Other countries and other burdens came to my mind, and I prayed for them, but even as I did, I kept apologizing to the Lord for being fickle toward the country He had given me as my special love. I didn't understand what was happening to me.

One day Sister Ruth asked me if I would like to ride into town with her, and I gladly accepted. We did a few errands, and on the way back to the mission house, she said to me, "Is there something you have been wanting to ask me about?"

That prospect startled me a little, but I quickly gathered myself. She was right. I did have something I had been wanting to ask her about. I couldn't understand this whole business about the vision. I told her about it, and even as I did, I felt very bad about the fact that I was not praying for Egypt as I had been and that I felt no more love for her.

She listened very carefully, and when I had finished, she laughed. "Well, Sister Jane," she said to me, "don't you know that when you leave one country and go to another, God lifts that former burden? The fact that He has opened another door, and a golden one at that, shows that He is opening a greater door of opportunity for you now. What He has done in Egypt is wonderful, but it is only the beginning. He is giving you a golden opportunity to carry His Good News into other nations as well."

She could sense that I was saddened by the idea of abandoning my first love, and she continued, "At some point, the Lord will probably allow you to go back to Egypt. That bolt was not shut. In the mean-time, don't worry about it. You haven't done anything wrong. Let God's desire satisfy your heart."

That word brought a great strength to my life. How good to know that I hadn't lost something important, that God was just lifting it for the time being, and that He had something even better in store for me! I was not to limit my vision to one part of the world. God had many other nations for me to embrace in the future.

The vision of the golden door proved to be true, of course. From Israel I went on to India and to a much broader ministry. The fading of my desire toward Egypt proved to be momentary, and each year, when I bought an around-the-world ticket for my next missionary trip, I would include Egypt in it. I wanted very much to go back there. But each time, the Lord would not permit me to return to Egypt. It was only after seven years had passed that I did eventually return, and my love for the land and its people again found release.

Still today, I have a great love for Egypt. She was, after all, my first love. I pray for her often. And I still get excited every time I think about going there. I am believing God for great things for Egypt and for her people.

Twenty-One

Standing on the Inside

My arrival in Jerusalem had been an occasion for much rejoicing, for me and for the believers there. Part of the great excitement of getting there was taking all the things the Lord had given me to carry out of Egypt. During my last two weeks in Egypt, the Lord had opened His storehouses to me, and I now went forth laden down with gifts for the people in Jerusalem. I carried material for new clothing for the ladies, shoes, boots and gowns, and dolls for the children. The Egyptian believers had also given a generous love gift of cash for the church in Jerusalem. Carrying blessing out of Egypt for God's people in Jerusalem was such a great joy for me!

I had been in Jerusalem only a few days, however, when I awoke one morning to find that my skin had turned yellow. I had contracted hepatitis somewhere on my journey. I knew that my back had been hurting for a while and that I had been feeling very weak, but I thought it was just tiredness because of my busy schedule. I had been preaching and teaching several times a day for the past six weeks. Now, I knew that my tiredness and my backache represented a much more serious threat.

Sister Ruth was very gracious to me. Some of the others wanted to put me in a room and lock me away to make sure no one else got the hepatitis, but she said no. "We're going to believe God for Sister Jane," she said that day in the prayer meeting. "She's going to come and pray with us every day, and God is going to heal her." I went every morning and added to my prayers a desperate plea for God to do a miracle for my health.

Usually, we all stood for the four hours of prayer each morning, but this now became very difficult for me. I was extremely tired, and it seemed that my back would break in two.

The four-hour morning prayer period was interrupted each day only by a tea break of some fifteen minutes at about ten o'clock. Everyone would get a cup of tea, and then we would go back to our prayer.

The tea break served more than one purpose. It was wintertime in Israel, and for the most part the houses were not heated. We had heat only in one room. Hot tea felt very good about ten in the morning because I was cold all the time.

One particular morning, when it came time for the tea break, I sat down near the fireplace to try to warm myself. I huddled as close to the fire as I could get. My back was hurting very badly. Sister Ruth looked over at me and said, "Sister Jane, it's all right if you sit down on the outside — as long as you're standing up on the inside." She said no more, and they were simple words, but this became a wonderful revelation for my life. Whatever I was suffering at the moment, I could stand tall on the inside and refuse to let it get me down, and God would carry me through.

That word kept me as I traveled through the nations in the coming years. Things would happen that would bring me low physically, but I would never be bowed in my spirit. I would always be standing up on the inside.

I suffered from the hepatitis over the next four weeks. One day we were all in the church, St. Peter-en-Gallicantu, for one of our regular meetings, and one of the main leaders in the group came to me and said, "The Lord has spoken to me that you should go home and go to bed." This was the last thing I wanted to hear. I had never been one to spend a lot of time in bed, and the idea of going to bed in the middle of the day did not appeal to me at all. Still, since she had put it like she did, I had to consider it. After we had eaten lunch, I did something I rarely do. I went to the room where I was staying and went to bed.

I was able to fall asleep, and I had a dream. In the dream, I was in a hospital undergoing surgery. I could see doctors gathered around working on me. Then I was taken into the recovery room. There in that recovery room, I saw the Lord standing at the end of my bed. He spoke just one word — "Recovery!" — and I suddenly woke up.

I thought back over that very vivid dream, and found that I could recall the details of it. That one powerful word — "Recovery!" — stuck in my mind. If someone is in the recovery room, I began to realize, that means that one has survived a surgical procedure and everything is all right.

From that moment on, I began to regain my strength, and within a week or so after that, I was fully recuperated from the hepatitis. The yellow was gone from my skin. My back had stopped aching. And I had a new lease on life.

By the time I left Jerusalem, I was a new person. I knew that I could face anything and that the Lord would deliver me.

Twenty-Two

The New Song

The day I had gone into town with Sister Ruth and she asked me if there was something I wanted to say to her, there had been something else on my mind other than the vision of the closing door for Egypt. The members of the group in Jerusalem had learned to sing spontaneously to the Lord, singing out a new song as it was given to them by the Spirit, and I just couldn't seem to do it. I told her, "By the time I get something to sing, you've already gone on to something else. Then, by the time I get something to go with what you're now singing, you've already moved on again. I just can't catch up."

The thing that bothered me most was that one of the leaders of the group had the habit of tapping me on the shoulder in prayer and saying, "Get a song," and I just couldn't seem to do it.

There was much more to it than I was admitting. I didn't have a good voice and had never been good with music, and I was afraid that if I sang, my song might pull the group down in the Spirit, and they would have to start all over again.

This whole affair was another reason that I was feeling miserable during the prayer meetings. Because I was trying so hard to come up with something to sing, I couldn't concentrate on what we were praying. Therefore, I wasn't enjoying the presence of the Lord.

After I had finished my long explanation of why I couldn't do what was expected of me and why that bothered me, Sister Ruth asked, "Do you want to sing spontaneously?"

I said, "Well, yes. I do want to, but I just can't."

She said, "If you have the desire, if you really want to, it will come."

The next morning, I went into the prayer time with a new attitude. I was no longer concentrating on singing a new song or on receiving a line of lyrics. I was determined to concentrate on the Lord and worship Him and not let anything disturb my spirit. I was never again going to be miserable in His presence. I would seek His face, and whatever happened would happen.

That's all it took. Within days after having this change of attitude, I was joining in with those who were singing spontaneously in the Spirit in the services. I was more amazed than anyone else when I suddenly began to sing forth a new phrase in the

Spirit one morning. This represented a great breakthrough in my life and the beginning of something wonderful, and I never looked back.

I can say to those who are reading this book, as Sister Ruth said to me, "If you want it badly enough, it will come." It is one of those gifts the Father delights to bestow on us.

Twenty-Three

Stepping Through the Golden Door

I stayed in Jerusalem longer than anticipated, and
during that time, God spoke to Sister Ruth to send
me to India. God had put a desire in my heart to
minister in that country again some time before this,
but I hadn't planned to go there on this particular
trip. When a sister from Bombay (Sister Mona) visited us in Jerusalem and extended an invitation to
the group, Sister Ruth felt that this was the time for
me to go. She obtained a one-month visa at the Indian consulate in Tel Aviv and a one-month
round-trip ticket to India, and I flew into Bombay
with Sister Mona.

I arrived in India with two pieces of luggage. One
of them was an accordion that Sister Ruth had asked
me to deliver to an Indian pastor, and the other was
a practically empty suitcase. Because it was wintertime in the Middle East, I had gone there with all
winter clothing. India, on the other hand, was hot,

and I had no proper clothes for that climate. I was believing God to supply for me while I was there.

Sister Mona took me to her house to spend the night, and I was planning to travel on to Chandigarh the following day to be with Pastor Samuel Johns, a good friend of Sister Ruth's for many years and a pioneer in his area. I also had to pass another town to leave the accordion.

I went to church with Sister Mona and met a lady there who was from the very city I needed to go to for the delivery of the accordion. She was going back home the next day, and she suggested that I accompany her on the train. Amazingly, when we arrived in her city, we found that the man I wanted to see lived just across the street from her house. She hadn't known it until we got there.

When I went to deliver the accordion, I found that there were three children in the pastor's home who had hepatitis. I had just been healed of it, and it was a great test of my faith to be exposed to the sickness again so soon. I delivered the accordion to the brother, and we had a time of fellowship.

This man was also related to Samuel Johns of Chandigarh, and when he knew that I was going there, he said to me, "It's too far for you to go from here. It's a journey of a day and a half, and you will arrive too late at night for anyone to meet you. It would be better if you went by way of New Delhi.

You could stop off there at the home of Pastor K.T. Thomas. He would be happy to receive you and give you a place to stay for the night. Then you can travel on the next day to Chandigarh." I accepted his suggestion.

Mona gave me some clothes, so my suitcase got a little heavier, and with it I boarded a train for New Delhi. I called Pastor K.T. Thomas from the train station in New Delhi, explaining to him who I was and why I had come to India. I told him I was on my way to Chandigarh and that the other pastor (also a relative of his) had recommended that I stay the night with him. He said he would come to pick me up.

When Pastor Thomas arrived at the train station, I received a shock. He had a long beard and flowing garments, and he was riding a motorcycle. To me, he looked like anything but a preacher. All I could think of was the appearance of the American hippies of the 1960s period, and I wasn't at all sure that I should get on the motorcycle with my suit case and go with him.

Was this man really who he said he was? I had to do some quick praying. In the end, God gave me peace about the situation. That was a relief because I didn't seem to have much of a choice at the moment. I didn't know anyone, and I was far from home. I was depending on other people, and I had to trust someone to help me.

As to hanging onto the motorcycle and juggling the suitcase at the same time, I had my doubts. The pastor agreed and rented a bicycle rickshaw to take the suitcase to his house. It was Good Friday when I arrived.

At Pastor Thomas' house, we sat and talked for several hours. He had many wonderful experiences to relate, and I was more than a little intimidated about being with a person who had had such wonderful experiences in God. The more he talked, the smaller I felt, until suddenly I just wanted to get out of there.

Pastor Thomas told me that his home was also used as a school of theology, and that didn't help my fears. I had already been feeling anxious, and now I was terrified. I barely knew what the word *theology* meant, and it sounded ominous to me.

I was taken to my room and finally got to bed that night, and the next morning I was introduced to some of the students. A little later in the morning, Pastor Thomas said to me, "Sister, it's too far to go to Chandigarh today. You'll arrive there too late for anyone to meet you at the train. You must go early in the day. If you can stay for our church service tomorrow, I will give you an opportunity to say a few words to the people."

I didn't really want to stay, but before I knew what I was saying, I had responded, "Okay," and then I wondered why.

I went up to my room, and before long, the pastor's daughter, Susan, came to the door. "Daddy said to tell you that he's going to arrange a special meeting for you tonight," she said. That news threw me into a whirl of emotion and prayer, as my brain began to work overtime. *Okay*, I thought, *he's going to have a small meeting for me tonight just so he can see if I have anything in God before he allows me to speak to the church in the morning.*

Susan said the meeting would be at the school. *Oh, my*, I thought, *they will all be theology students.* I had discovered that some of the "theology students" had been pastors already for many years and were just returning for additional training. *What have I gotten myself into?* I was wondering.

As soon as Susan left, I moved the little bed up against the door and put a chair against the bed to make sure nobody came into the room while I called out desperately to God. It was 1:00 p.m., and my plea rose up to Heaven.

I was afraid to pray in English for fear that I would pray doubt, so I decided that the best thing I could do was pray in other tongues. I did that, from one o'clock that afternoon until six o'clock that evening, without ceasing — out loud. I laughed and I cried, but I poured out my soul to God.

At six o'clock I took a shower and dressed. Then someone brought me a cup of tea. And suddenly it was time to go downstairs for the meeting.

Now I was feeling much better. Between one and six, something had happened. I may have heard the teaching that praying in the Spirit edifies us, but the reality of it hadn't totally sunk in until that day. Suddenly, I realized that I was not nearly as nervous as I had been before. I felt strangely confident.

The meeting was opened with prayer, and soon Pastor Thomas introduced me. No sooner had I begun to speak than the Lord began to give me words of knowledge for those present. Three people fell out of their seats as I called them out, and God healed them. He filled others with the Holy Spirit while I was speaking. Toward the end of my time, I called the whole group forward to receive the Holy Spirit. Ninety-five percent of the students of the school of theology received the baptism of the Holy Spirit that night, and every one of them was slain in the Spirit and lay in God's presence on the floor. What a marvelous meeting we had!

The next day I was given twenty minutes to speak to the whole church. Although a preacher had already been designated for that special service, it is not unusual in India to have several

144

special speakers in any one service. We had a wonderful time that day.

Pastor Thomas came to me after the service and asked me if I would be willing to stay on for a week to conduct some special services. For the first three nights, he said, he would invite no outsiders, just his church people. He wanted them to be ministered to. Then, after that, they could bring in others.

These meetings were so successful and God did so many miracles that one week turned into two, and two weeks turned into three, until I was actually there in New Delhi with Pastor Thomas and his people for about two months.

After one entire week with the church, Pastor Thomas moved the meetings outdoors. He had not done any advertising or any extensive planning, but many hundreds of people came and received Christ as their Savior, were healed and were filled with the Spirit. During the daytime, Pastor Thomas took me on the back of his motorcycle out to many other surrounding places to preach.

I have been able to go back to visit the church in New Delhi several times through the years, and it is wonderful what God has done there. I have also had meetings with some of the other pastors who were studying in New Delhi at the time. They are great people of faith who have done wonderful things for the Kingdom.

After all these years, I'm still on my way to Chandigarh. I've never gotten there yet, and I also have never yet had the privilege of meeting Pastor Samuel Johns. I trust that I will do that on this side of Heaven. In the meantime, the outpouring of the Spirit in New Delhi had been too important to leave.

Twenty-Four

No Visa, No Ticket and No Money

Because my visa to India had been good only for one month, it became necessary to extend it while I was there in New Delhi. Pastor Thomas made the proper inquiries, filed a request for a one-month extension and then took me in for a personal interview. The first person we talked to told us it couldn't be done; India welcomed tourists, but not Christian missionaries. I was sent to another official and another and another, shuttling from office to office in this way for several days.

In one office, the official actually threw my passport at me and told me that there was no way I could stay longer. Then he sent me on to another office.

Eventually, the case was pushed up to a much higher authority, and I was called in for questioning. "What do you do?" the foreign affairs officer asked me.

I knew I needed wisdom in that moment. If I told him what I actually did, there was no way he could extend my visa. "I work at a lost-and-found place," I said. "It's a camp where people who are lost come and find themselves."

He turned and looked me in the eye. "You're a Christian?" he asked.

"Yes, sir, I am," I told him.

He said, "I can tell by the way you're dressed. Many foreigners come here dressed skimpily. You have covered yourself well." (I had on a long skirt and a long-sleeved blouse that day.) We talked for a few more minutes, and then he stamped my visa with a one-month extension. God had seen my need and helped me.

Long before it came time to leave India, I realized that the expiration date on my airline ticket had already passed. I had decided not to say anything to Pastor Thomas or to any of his people. God had led me to stay, and I didn't want them to feel obligated financially. Although they were graciously providing my room and board, there were no offerings in the meetings as we are accustomed to in the West. I had been away from home for about four months, and my money was about gone. I had no idea what a ticket back to Jerusalem would cost, but I was trusting that God would provide whatever I needed.

The Lord showed me when it was time to leave New Delhi, and I made my good-byes and caught a train for Bombay. Arriving in Bombay on a Friday night, I was welcomed by Sister Mona into her home once again. After we had talked for a while, I went to the little room where I stayed and began to pray seriously about this matter of my ticket. Time was running out, and I urgently needed an answer.

There were several complications. My visa would run out on Monday, my ticket was expired, and I had very little money left. I decided not to bother Sister Mona with these details but to take them only to the Lord. Trusting God for something so critical and serious was a new experience for me, and I prayed all night.

The next morning, Sister Mona mentioned that she had heard me praying in the night and wondered if anything was wrong. I told her that I needed to go to the airport to see about my ticket. She said that these things were done in town at the airline office, but that she doubted that anyone would be there on Saturday. "We'll go on Monday," she said.

I went back to my room, but before long God spoke to me and said, "No, go today."

I went back downstairs and said, "Sister Mona, the Lord just spoke to me that I should go today."

"Then, let's go," she said.

She had someone go and get her driver, and he readied the car and then drove us into the city. We located the office of that particular airline, but it seemed to be closed. Fortunately, it was only closed for lunch. Afterward, an agent returned.

I asked him what it would cost to fly to Jerusalem. "It's five hundred and thirty-eight dollars," I was told by the agent. "But Ma'am," he continued, "even if I could sell you a ticket today, you wouldn't get out of here for the next fifteen days. We're booked full until then."

"But you don't understand," I protested. "My visa is about to expire. Monday is my last day to be in this country."

"I'm very sorry," he replied. "There is nothing we can do about that."

He asked to see my passport, and when I pulled it out, the expired ticket fell out too. "Oh, but you have a ticket!" he said.

"Well, I do," I said, "but it has expired. It was a thirty-day ticket, and so it's no longer valid."

He examined the ticket very carefully, and while he did, another man came in and sat down to my left. After a while, the agent threw the ticket back on the counter in front of me and said, "This ticket is no good."

I said, "Yes, sir. That's what I was telling you."

But then I saw something change in his eyes. Without a word, he picked up the ticket again and reexamined it. Then he said, "The man sitting next to you is the person you need to talk to. He's the representative of the company you bought this ticket from," and he said something to the man.

The man introduced himself to me. He said his name was Abraham Moses.

I explained to him my situation. I had another ticket that I had left in Jerusalem that would take me back to Virginia from there, but I needed to get back to Jerusalem, and my permission to be in India was running out.

He looked at my ticket, and he examined my passport. He asked me several questions about the visa stamps I had there. Then he asked, "Have you been sick?"

I told him I hadn't.

"Yet you stayed over an extra month. Why did you stay so long?"

I said, "Because I wanted to see more of your country while I was here."

"Well," he said, "there's nothing I can do about the ticket, but I may be able to help you with your visa."

It suddenly dawned on me that this man was Jewish, and I said to him, "Mister Abraham Moses, I am believing and trusting the same God that you trust in. My Bible tells me that He is a miracle-working God, and I believe in miracles. I'm believing for a miracle now."

"Come and go with me to our office, and we'll

151

see if there's anything we can do to help you," he said. We walked with him to his office.

After some deliberations with his staff, Abraham Moses said, "It's just as I thought. We cannot do anything about the ticket, but I think we can get you a fifteen-day extension on your visa. Leave all your papers with us, and I'll call you tomorrow at twelve o'clock to let you know what we find out." I gave him my passport and the expired ticket, and Sister Mona and I went back home.

By eleven o'clock the next morning, I was already staying near the phone. But no call came.

Twelve o'clock came and went, and there was no call.

Mister Abraham Moses didn't call at one o'clock, two o'clock, three o'clock, four o'clock or five o'clock.

By this time, I was feeling very foolish. I was in a strange country, and I had given all of my travel documents to a total stranger. Now I had no ticket, no passport, no visa, no record of coming into the country and no record of the extension of my permission to stay in the country. I didn't even have any form of identification. I was about to become an illegal alien — without any papers at all. What a mess I had gotten myself into!

With these thoughts, my prayer suddenly shifted into high gear. I prayed all night again. Mona wondered why I was doing this, but I still hadn't told her that I had no money to buy a ticket. I didn't have money — PERIOD!

Early the next morning a sister came to the house. She was the wife of one of the local movie directors, but she was a wonderful Christian, and we had met in a prayer meeting. She said the Lord had spoken to her to bring me a gift of a hundred and twenty-five rupees. I was delighted to receive the money, but I was more delighted and deeply touched to realize that God had His people there in Bombay who could respond to His voice and help me.

Less than an hour had passed when another sister came, and she, too, said that the Lord had spoken to her to bring me an offering. Her offering was a hundred rupees. How blessed I was to think that God would be so concerned about my need that He would speak to local people to give to me in this way!

We had often been taught in camp that the only person we needed to tell about our needs was the Lord, and I was finding that this was very true. I hadn't told anyone else about my predicament, and yet God was working through His people.

A short time later, another person came with a similar story and gave me fifty rupees. I now had two hundred and seventy-five rupees (equivalent to about thirty-three dollars), but that was far from the five hundred and thirty-eight dollars I needed.

The morning passed, and still there was no call from Abraham Moses. This was my final day of permission in the country, and what would I do next if he didn't come through?

At about one o'clock the phone rang, and it was for me. "Sarah Jane," the voice on the other end of the line said, "this is Abraham Moses. I need to tell you that God has done a miracle. Are you sitting down or standing up?"

"I'm standing up," I said.

"Well, you'd better sit down," he replied.

Thinking about it later, I wonder if I had even heard the word *miracle*. If I had, it hadn't rung a bell. When Abraham Moses suggested that I sit down, I thought something terrible had happened. I quickly sat down, and braced myself for bad news.

"Sarah," he continued, "tonight at one o'clock, you will be flying out of here."

Oh, my, I thought, *if I'm to fly out of here tonight, that means I need the five hundred and thirty-eight dollars, and I need it now.*

"How much was that ticket?" I asked, hoping against hope that it had somehow become cheaper overnight.

He said, "You didn't understand me. I told you God has done a miracle."

154

"I understand," I said. "You were able to get me on the flight, but I'm concerned about how much it will cost."

He said, "God has done a miracle."

For some reason, what he was saying still wasn't registering in my brain. All I could think of was five hundred and thirty-eight dollars, and it seemed like five hundred and thirty-eight thousand dollars at the moment. I needed it, and I didn't have it. This man had convinced someone to allow me to fly, but how could I pay for the flight?

He repeated, "Sarah, God has done a miracle." Then he explained, "You're flying on your old ticket. There is no charge."

"Did you say, 'No charge'?" I asked.

"No charge!" he assured me. "God has done a miracle, and you're flying on your old ticket. There will be no charge whatsoever."

It finally sank into my consciousness that the miracle I had been believing for had become a reality. God had provided a way for me to get back to Israel, and it wasn't going to cost me anything at all.

"Well, that's wonderful," I said to Abraham Moses, "but surely I owe you something for your services. How much do I owe *you*?" The amount he told me was less than fifty rupees, and the Lord had graciously provided it that very morning. I would be able to give him twice what he was asking and still have plenty left over to pay my airport tax and to bless those who had been washing my clothes and cooking my meals at Sister Mona's house. How wonderful the Lord is!

When Abraham Moses tried to explain to me where to meet him at eight o'clock that night at a certain service station on a certain road, I put Mona on the phone because I was unfamiliar with the streets. She took down the directions and told him we would be there to meet him at the appointed time. We were there before eight anxiously waiting.

Eight o'clock came and went.

Eight-thirty ...

Eight-forty-five ...

Nine o'clock ...

Nine-fifteen ...

Nine-thirty ...

Nine-forty-five came and went, and still no one came.

Now, my thoughts ran wild. *This is a story right out of some book,* my mind told me. *The man is not going to show up, and everything I have prayed and believed for is lost. What will I do now?* But I kept believing God.

It was nearly ten o'clock when Abraham Moses finally arrived. As we stood there in that parking lot and he placed the revalidated ticked and my passport and visa into my hand, it was like a dream come true. God was faithful. He does provide. At that moment, a new faith was birthed into my heart. I suddenly knew that I could go anywhere and do anything for God, and my every need *would* be supplied.

Only after I had everything in my hand did I dare tell Sister Mona and the rest of her family what God had done. Until then, they didn't know that I had no money to buy a ticket. The Indian people had been so gracious and hospitable to me that the thought of putting pressure on them to somehow supply my financial need had grieved my spirit. Now I knew that I never needed to depend on people anywhere. It was a wonderful moment that would change my life forever and open new doors to me in the future.

It was another great miracle just to get back to Sister Mona's house, get my luggage into the car and get to the airport in time to catch my flight out that night. What a wonderful, wonderful, wonderful journey it had been!

There was another great miracle. The suitcase I had brought in two months before was now full. So many things had been given to me personally and other things for me to take back to the ministry in Jerusalem that I couldn't carry them all. I had to leave some things with Sister Mona to take with her the next time she traveled to Jerusalem.

I got back to Israel just as the group was ending a forty-day fast. I stayed another ten days with them and then went back to Virginia. The future was looking very bright!

Twenty-Five

Favor With God and Man

The first time I went to Taiwan, several of us ladies had embarked on an around-the-world trip. It was Debbie Jones, Margaret Cummings and myself. Remarkably, we left home with only a little more than seventy dollars each in our pockets, so we were immediately thrust upon the mercies of God.

Our itinerary was planned to include Hawaii, Japan, Taiwan, Hong Kong, Mainland China, Korea, the Philippines and Nepal. How we would go so many places on less than two hundred and fifty dollars we didn't know, but we knew that God had spoken to us to do it. We had no idea of exactly how much we might need in each country for airport tax, so we were not buying any food. If no one invited us to eat, we fasted.

We didn't know anyone in Taiwan, but while we were in Hawaii, someone gave me the name of a Taiwanese pastor, Peter Chu. They said he was a very good brother and that if we would get in touch with him, he would surely want us to minister in his church. They gave us his telephone number.

It was late when we arrived in Taipei, so we got a hotel room for the night. When we woke up the next morning, Margaret was very sick, too sick to get out of bed.

We tried to call Pastor Chu from the hotel, but we couldn't reach anyone who spoke good English. The lady who answered seemed to be telling us that Pastor Chu was not pastoring there anymore, so Debbie and I went out on the streets of the city and walked for the next six or seven hours, praying as we went. It was not a matter of staying or not staying. It was a matter of finding out what God wanted us to do. We had a ticket onward, but if the Lord wanted us in Taiwan, He would open doors for us and provide for our needs.

After some seven hours of prayer, I said to the others, "I'm going to try one more time to reach Pastor Chu. If we can't reach him, then we must move on. We'll pack our bags, get to the airport and go on to Hong Kong."

I again dialed the number we had been given. This time, the lady answering spoke very good English. She told us that Pastor Chu was in a far mountain fasting and praying for three days. He was believing God for revival in his church.

I told her who we were and that God had spoken to us to come.

"Who told you?" she asked.

"God told us to come," I repeated.

She said she would contact Pastor Chu and call us back.

Within a few minutes, we received the call: "Cathy will be coming to pick you up for the service."

Margaret was still in bed, not feeling any better, but I said to her, "We need to get ready for church." We had been taught in camp never to stay home sick when we had an opportunity to get to a service. The best place to be healed was always in the presence of the Lord. And we practiced that simple truth.

But Margaret was very sick. She said, "I'm not going."

I said, "You have to get up. We're not going without you."

She said, "I just can't."

I said, "Get up, and get your clothes on. We are *all* going. And God is going to heal you in the service."

She managed to get up and get dressed, and we were ready when the time came to meet Cathy in the lobby. When Cathy came in, we were delighted to see that she was someone we knew. We had known her as Ling Ling. I had met her in Israel, and

Margaret knew her, too. This helped break the ice for us that night.

We were told before the service by the assistant pastor that he would give each of us an opportunity to give a testimony in the service. When the time came, Margaret gave her testimony first, and she was completely healed. Next, Debbie gave her testimony. Then it was my turn.

Brother Heflin had always told us to keep our testimonies short, and that night we were very short. I said only a few words, and then I turned the service back over to the assistant pastor. He came to the microphone, but he seemed hesitant. He looked at us and said, "Would you please just take the service tonight." So we did.

Many received the baptism of the Holy Spirit that night and were slain in the Spirit. It was well worth a trip to Taiwan just to see that happen.

We went back to our hotel room that night with the idea that we would get our things together and leave the next morning. Before long, however, we received a phone call. It was Pastor Chu. He said, "I heard what happened in the church tonight. This is what I've been praying for. Would you please stay for three more days and minister in the church."

I said, "I would love to. Let me ask the other two what they feel." I didn't have a problem with staying, but my concern was that we didn't have enough money to stay on in the hotel. He hadn't said anything about taking care of our expenses, so I wasn't sure what we should tell him. If we spent all our money in one place, how could we complete our around-the-world trip?

I said to the others, "Pastor Chu wants us to stay for a few days. What do you feel? "

They answered, "Whatever you say, we'll do."

I said, "Well, I really feel that God would have us to stay, but the thing is that we don't have enough money to pay our own expenses. Pray quickly and see what the Lord shows you."

No one said anything. I still felt that we should stay, so I said to Pastor Chu, "We'll stay for the three days."

Before we could get to bed that night, the telephone rang again. It was Pastor Chu. "I forgot to say that we'll take care of all of your expenses — the hotel and your food. You have nothing to worry about." What a relief that was! We slept very well that night.

We were in Pastor Chu's church for twenty-one days and had meetings every night. New people were coming to every service. Later, Pastor Chu opened many wonderful doors for us, not only around Taiwan, but also in Malaysia, Singapore, Indonesia and Australia.

Twenty-Six

Trekking in the Himalayas

Several things worked together to give me a great burden for Nepal. Sister Ruth had spent time there in the early 1960s and had received a wonderful open door to the royal family. She had returned several times and had done extensive Gospel distribution in that formerly closed nation. She often related wonderful stories of the spiritual hunger of the Nepali people.

Then Brother Charles Mendies (son of a Canadian missionary lady and her Indian husband living in Kathmandu) had come and lived with us for a time in the camp in Ashland. He was such a loving and dedicated brother that he became like a son to all of us. I was looking forward to visiting his country.

Nepal had been a strong Hindu country for many years, and there were laws against preaching the Gospel, distributing tracts and winning someone to Christ. Quite a number of Christians had been imprisoned for being baptized. The sentence was one year. If those doing the baptizing were caught, they were sentenced to seven years. Charles had once been detained, and his wife Susan was detained as well. But the Gospel must be preached to all men everywhere.

We had told Charles that we wanted to do some trekking in the mountains. Tourists found the Himalayas fascinating, and trekking to isolated mountain villages gave us a wonderful opportunity to preach and hand out gospels of John. He agreed to accompany us.

We began our trip inside the country with a long bus ride out from the capital city. We boarded the bus at nine o'clock one night and arrived at the end of the line at five the next morning. The bus could go no further, for there were no more roads. It was all walking from there. We paused long enough to get a cup of tea and refresh ourselves, and then we started on our way.

We had not come well prepared for the trek. The special shoes we picked up for the purpose were cheap and flimsy, and our feet suffered terribly as a consequence. We walked all that first day, arriving at our destination about six o'clock that night. Still, we were ready to have a service there at seven-thirty.

The glory of God came on that mountain and re-moved the tiredness from our bodies so that we could speak and minister. The next day we were ready to go on.

Trekking in the Himalayas

At one point, we lost the trail because of a land-slide and became disoriented. Consequently, what should have been a three-hour hike turned into an eight-hour hike. Our guide didn't tell us until later that we had been hopelessly lost, and only the Lord helped us find our way. Through it all, we were able to keep moving only because of the anointing. The Lord Himself walked with us.

With all of her challenges, I loved Nepal, and over the next several years, I took teams there each year for this trekking ministry. One year, we took a group of ten and Charles joined us to other groups (one of them was from Elim Bible College, for example). Altogether we had forty men and women on that trip. We formed into ten teams, and each team was sent in a different direction. At other times, we all moved together.

On that particular trip, I was the leader of our group, and we were to spend the next twenty-one days trekking through the mountains, carrying gospels of John and wind-up cassette tape players with taped versions of the Bible on them for those who could not read. In every village, we would give out our gospels of John or one of the tape players. In a few villages, we felt it was not safe to give anything, so we just stopped for a cup of tea and a snack before moving on.

There was always a place in each village (we called

them Nepali truck stops) where two stone pillars had been erected with a stone cross beam seated on them. The beam sat at just the right height for bearers to rest their heavy burdens on. When we came to these places, we let our backpacks rest against the "burden bearer" for a little while, as we regained our strength.

The work we were doing was very dear to the heart of God, and we were attacked by the enemy in many different ways. For example, one of the young ladies in my team broke her leg, and we were forced to carry her for the next five days. To say that this wasn't easy is an understatement. The hiking was difficult enough, without the extra burden of another person. Plus, we now had to carry her backpack as well as our own.

This arrangement wasn't easy for her either. She had to exercise great faith and trust us not to let her drop down the steep sides of the mountains.

We alternated between carrying her in one of two ways. Sometimes one person would carry her piggyback, but most of the time two of us carried her on a kind of stretcher we made with two poles. We thus wrestled with her weight as we wound our way up and down mountains and crossed rivers and rice paddies.

It was a new experience for all of us, and we met God in new and wonderful ways, as He sustained us. We needed His supernatural strength, we needed

His loving compassion and we needed His joy. This was definitely not fun!

Our goal had been to get the lady with the broken led to a point where we could find a bus to send her back to Kathmandu. It would normally have taken us three days to reach that place. Instead, it took us five days.

When we reached the place where a bus passed for the capital, I became concerned. Would everyone want to go back when they had the chance? I had a serious talk with the Lord because I wondered if this might mean the end of a mission for which we had all sacrificed so much.

"What do I say to my teammates," I prayed, "to convince them to go on?" I would have understood if any one of them or every one of them had decided to turn back. They were all very tired. They had terrible blisters on their feet. They had been bitten by leeches from the rivers we crossed. And they were tired of eating nothing but Magi instant noodles. Turning back had to be a great temptation to all of them. What could I say to convince them otherwise?

"This is what I want you to say to them," the Lord answered. "We've been presented with the possibility of turning back. You can choose to do that, or you can choose to go on and finish the course. As for me, I'm going on. I want to finish what we started."

I had fallen a little behind, so I caught up with the

169

group and found them all lying down on their back-packs, obviously exhausted. Was my little speech hopeless? I told them exactly what the Lord had said to me, and then I looked from face to face to see what their reaction would be.

The one who spoke up first said, "I'm going with you, Boss." Then others chimed in, "Me too," until everyone was accounted for. Not one of the group turned back.

While our guide took the lady with the broken leg back to Kathmandu, it gave the rest of us a break. We had to bed down and wait until he got back. He got the sister to the capital (it was three more days before she could see a doctor). He ate something, and then he turned around and caught another bus back to where we were waiting for him. Such dedication!

All forty of us lost fifteen or twenty pounds or more during that trek. It was arduous work, but it was worth it all. We were able to distribute many gospels of John, and through them, thousands of Nepalis came to a knowledge of the Lord Jesus Christ. There are now many churches spread through those Himalayan mountains and at least a hundred thousand Christian believers are reported to exist in the little country of Nepal. Thank God for the grace and glory that came to us in those days and kept us moving forward for Him.

Twenty-Seven

Through the Valley of the Shadow of Death

Many of us became ill on that trip — from altitude sickness and from the impure food and water. I became *very* ill myself. When we got back to Kathmandu, I was so sick that I couldn't keep anything down — not even water. This severe nausea persisted for several days.

I had a difficult schedule ahead and would not be going back home for many months. I was due next for meetings in India. So each day I spent several hours in prayer, and each day I tried to eat something to regain my strength. One morning, however, not long after I had eaten some toast with peanut butter on it, I was walking in the fresh air in the flower garden when I fainted. Later, when I began to come to, I remembered having been in the flower garden and didn't know how I had gotten back upstairs to my room. Someone had evidently carried me.

One of the sisters from our team was there, and

she was speaking to me, but her voice seemed to be a thousand miles away. I finally realized that she was reading from the Bible:

> *The LORD is my shepherd;*
> *I shall not want.*
> *He maketh me to lie down in green pastures.*

She later went on to read other portions of scripture, and I heard her, but I couldn't speak. I seemed to have no life in me, and everyone considered that I was unconscious. As much as I wanted to, I couldn't pray.

When she got to the part that said, *"Yea, though I walk through the valley of the shadow of death, I will fear no evil; for thou art with me; thy rod and thy staff they comfort me,"* I had a vision. I saw some rough, black waters, and on the waters I saw a very tiny ship. As the waters swelled upward, they would overflow the ship, and I saw that the weight of the water was pushing the tiny ship to the bottom.

Then, I saw a tiny pinpoint of light on the ship. As the ship went down and came back up several times, I saw that same pinpoint of light. Then I saw a passageway through the water and knew that if the little ship could get out through that passageway, it would be safe on the other side.

Suddenly, I realized that I was that tiny ship and

that the pinpoint of light inside of me was Jesus. He was with me in this turmoil, even though I was incapable of calling His name. I realized what it means to go through *"the valley of the shadow of death"* and to be so helpless that I could not even call out to God. It was so dark that I could not see His face, yet that tiny spark of light was still burning within me and would bring me back to the top each time the water would try to drag me down.

Then, I sensed that the light was guiding my ship through a passage out of there. I can still see it today. There were jagged rocks on every side, and it was obviously a very dangerous passage. At the same time, I sensed that on the other side of that dangerous passage, great peace and beauty waited.

The light was pushing me up through the water and out through the passage. The Lord had promised to be my Shepherd, to lead me into green pastures and beside still waters, to take me to where His table was spread. My enemy was clearly anticipating a victory over me, but God was about to spread a table before me in the presence of my enemy. I would sit down to eat, and the enemy's plan would be foiled. God would arise in my life, and my enemies would be scattered.

When my ship went through the opening, I suddenly regained consciousness. My companion told me that she had been reading to me for two hours.

God had brought me through that terrible *"valley of the shadow of death."*

I still wasn't well, and it would have been easy for me to go home at that moment. No one would have blamed me if I had, but God told me to go on to India, and I would see His salvation, so I went.

Although I still wasn't feeling well in India, day by day my strength increased, and I was able to finish my ministry there before returning home.

Whatever the "bug" was that I picked up in Nepal, it stayed with me for a long time. Nine months later, although I still wasn't well, I returned to Nepal. It was actually about a year before I was completely free of that thing. In the meantime, everywhere I went, God sent revival. Everywhere I went, people were saved and healed and set free. Blind eyes were opened, and deaf ears heard again. Where would I have been during those months without the Good Shepherd?

There is one more important footnote to that particular Nepali trip. After we got back to Kathmandu, some went on to India and the Philippines, and those of us who remained behind began to go out into the Kathmandu Valley, doing the same work there we had done in the mountain villages. This proved to be much more dangerous.

One evening we noticed that our men, Phil Meager and Kenny Barr, had not returned. We soon learned that they had been arrested and put in jail for the distribution of Christian materials. We set about seeking God in prayer, and the next day Charles began to make all the contacts among the resident diplomats he could, trying to find someone who could intervene before the Nepali government on behalf of the two men.

The situation did not look hopeful. I was determined to stay there and continue praying until they were released. After spending three nights in prison, Phil and Kenny were indeed freed (although they were immediately sent out of the country). How good God is to us!

Twenty-Eight

Gathering Strength

I struggled for a long while with the title the Lord had put on me when Dr. Ward first prophesied to me in the restaurant that I would go forth to evangelize the nations. When the Lord sent me to the Philippines, for instance, and the people asked me if I was an evangelist or teacher or just what I considered myself to be, I would insist, "I'm just Sister Jane." I didn't want to go further than that. I was afraid to. Then one day, the Lord rebuked me for my attitude.

Janet Cooper and I were high up in the Philippine mountains, and one day we were praying together overlooking a beautiful mountain town. The Lord said to me, "You have not yet dared to call yourself what I have already called you. I told you through Dr. Ward that you would be an evangelist and travel the nations of the world, and still you refuse to let the word evangelist enter your mouth."

Boy, was He right! The word *EVANGELIST*

seemed awfully big to me, much TOO big, and I couldn't bring myself to say it — about myself at least. When I thought of an evangelist, I thought of Billy Graham, so I had never allowed myself to use the term. I felt that if I started saying that I was an evangelist, I would have too much to live up to, and I wasn't sure I was up to the task. I was certainly no Billy Graham.

"But evangelizing," the Lord told me that day, "is nothing more than speaking and teaching and declaring that I am the Lord and what I have done to bring salvation to man. It's what you have been doing for Me already. As you go and tell, the Spirit of evangelism will go with you, and many people will be saved, set free, healed and made whole." From that moment on, I had a new understanding of what God was doing in my life.

That night the local meeting place was packed, and people were crowded around the doors and windows looking in. Inside, the people were packed so tightly that it was difficult to move about. A young man who was sitting down inside had a scarf tied around his face, much like the Lone Ranger. I called him out and said, "Lone Ranger, come here." He came forward.

I reached out to touch him, but he said, "Don't touch me." (He didn't say it in English, but my interpreter let me know what was said.)

I was a little taken aback by this and wondered why the boy didn't want to be touched, but I said, "Okay, I won't touch you. I'll pray for you from a distance."

I prayed for him, and suddenly his arms went up and began to move up and down. Then he began to jump, and he was weeping.

"What happened?" I asked my interpreter.

She said, "I don't know."

He was saying something as he jumped, and eventually she understood that he was saying, "I'm healed." Later we learned the story. He had been suffering from many boils over his body — under his arms, on the inside of his legs and on his back — and God had instantly healed him.

"I didn't want you to touch me," he said, "because I hadn't been able to stand for anyone to touch me for a very long time."

We had a wonderful, wonderful meeting that night. The glory of God came, and people were saved, set free and made whole. I was accomplishing the work of an evangelist and gaining strength and boldness as I went.

In Egypt, a man asked me if I would pray for all of his children and friends. He got them all together in his house and lined them up around the wall. I started around the wall praying for each one of them and prophesying over them as I went. When I reached a young man at the back door, he said to me, "Don't pray for me."

I said, "Okay, I won't," and I kept on going around the walls of the house, ministering to others.

When I had prayed for everyone else, I felt that God was quickening something on the inside of me to say to that young man. I had never done anything like this before, but I pointed at him and spoke out the words God was giving me. "You shall not sleep another night until you come to know the Lord Jesus Christ as your Savior. No more sleep! I can pray for you from afar off."

He wasn't at the service that night, but the next night there was a note on the pulpit from him, asking if I would come to his house and pray for him. I didn't have time that night, and the next night there was another note waiting for me. He wasn't able to come to the service, it said. Could I please find time after the service to come to his house and pray for him. That night I was able to go.

When I arrived at the house, I found him seated. "You must pray for me," he said. "I haven't been able to sleep since you pointed your finger at me and prayed." That night, he was saved and filled with the Holy Ghost. After that, he traveled with us around Egypt for five weeks and opened many doors for my ministry.

I was learning that if I would get out of the way

and let God work, He would bring the increase. It is God who saves, God who delivers, God who heals. I was just His agent.

On one of my trips to Taiwan, I ministered in a Presbyterian church. I noticed that most of the people in the audience were very reserved. There were hardly any young people among them. Even my interpreter was a man in his seventies. He was a good enough interpreter, but we needed some life in the service.

The songs they sang were very formal, and all the proceedings were very staid and proper. When they handed me the microphone, I took off running across the front of the church laughing loudly. That got their attention.

Then the interpreter followed me and did everything I did. Within ten minutes every person in that meeting was dancing before the Lord. We had a grand time that day, and nearly everyone in the congregation was baptized in the Holy Ghost as the power of God and the presence of His being came into that place. Even the interpreter received the Holy Ghost.

God was giving me a boldness that caused me to do things I wouldn't normally do, and in the process, His presence was being revealed.

I suddenly realized that I had stopped caring about making a fool of myself. If God was going to get the glory, I didn't care what people thought about me. I could run and leap and do anything else God showed me to do, knowing that He was running and leaping with me, and that He would use my prophetic acts to set people free. We had a wonderful time in that place and in many other places in Taiwan.

On one trip to the Philippines, I was riding in a truck when the Lord began to give me a burden for one of the young men who was also in the truck. He was an American, but his appearance was very disheveled. He had very long blond hair and he had on long earrings. During my times of prayer over the coming days, I brought him before the Lord.

On the next Sunday night, I looked for him in the service, but he wasn't there. The church was filled, and people were standing outside looking in the windows and gathered around the door. During the altar call, I said to one of my companions, "I don't see that young man, but I'm going to find him. You keep the service going, and I'm going outside to look for him."

I asked the pastor, "Where is that young man?"

He said, "He's in the truck asleep."

I marched out of the church, praying for people as I went. I prayed for people in the yard as I passed them, and they were slain in the Spirit, but I pressed on toward the truck.

I climbed up on the running board and looked inside. "Hey!" I said, "What do you mean sleeping when we're having church? Get up and come out here." He complied. I hadn't given him a choice.

When he stepped down from the truck, I said to him, "God shows me that you're the son of a pastor and that you're backslidden, not serving God. But you have a great call on your life." With that, the young man melted. He dropped to his knees right there and invited Jesus back into his heart. He was slain in the Spirit for some forty-five minutes there in the moonlight under the trees, as God worked a great miracle in his life, brought him back into fellowship and baptized him in the Holy Ghost. It was wonderful!

I was becoming increasingly bold and doing more and more unusual things for God, and as I did, He was revealing His glory.

When our friend Charles Mendies was imprisoned in Nepal for his faith, he was sentenced to seven years. We all prayed much for his release, and I sensed that I should visit him and believe for God to do a miracle. At the same time I was terrified that I might do or say something that would only complicate his plight.

On one particular trip into that part of the world, my companion, Mary Wagner, and I were scheduled to go into India, but we had not planned to go on to Nepal. We joined Brother Heflin and his team for a crusade in Kenya, however, and when the people who were with him heard about Charles' imprisonment, they gave us an offering to enable us to fly into Kathmandu. This same thing happened in India.

In each of those places, I also received a recurring vision of the head of a snake. Its eyes were memorable. Its mouth was open, and I could see down its throat. It looked as if it was ready to strike. I wasn't sure if God was telling us that we were in immediate danger, or if the vision had some other meaning.

We went on to Nepal, and when we arrived there, the Lord showed me that the recurring vision of the snake was for Charles. I saw it again, but this time there was an added dimension. I saw a hand with a firm grip just at the back of the head of the snake, so that it was paralyzed in that position. It could not move, and it could not strike. God was telling me to assure Charles that the enemy could do him no harm and that within days, he would be released.

What a joy it was to be able to communicate this vision to Charles. Although it hurt me to see him behind bars, and a big lump would form in my throat, I was sure that he would soon be free.

We were warned that our conversations in the prison were monitored and that we should say nothing of Jesus and nothing of the Bible, so what we were able to share was very limited. On our way out of the country, we were to have one more opportunity, and I prayed that God would give me wisdom to know just what to say that would encourage Charles.

As I was standing before the bars again, a big lump formed in my throat, and I felt like crying. I didn't think I could say anything in that moment. Then the Lord said to me, "Ask Charles if he remembers the lowly Man of Galilee."

I got very excited because I realized that God was giving me the solution. If I could say something that only he would understand, we could communicate. I said, "Charles, do you remember the lowly Man of Galilee?"

He said, "Oh, yes, I remember."

"Well, He says to tell you that not many days from now, you're going to be released."

Then the Lord said to me, "Ask him if he remembers Brother Jude."

I said, "Charles, do you remember Brother Jude?"

"Oh, yes!" he said, "I remember him."

I said, "Well, he says to tell you to keep on praying in the Most High, building yourself up on your most holy faith" (Charles had memorized Jude 20 as a child, and at the Lord's direction, I was encouraging him to pray in the Spirit).

We said a few more things, and then it was time

to leave for the airport. On the way, I rejoiced at the awesome way God had allowed us to communicate. How great He was to put just the right words in my mouth!

By the time we got back home to Virginia, Charles had already been released from the prison. His family members had prepared themselves to see him serve out his entire seven-year sentence, as Christians before him had done, but God had another plan.

Little by little, I was gathering strength in my ministry, and now I felt great liberty. I knew that God was sending me each time I went out, I knew that He was with me, I knew that He would provide for me, I knew that He would keep me well and otherwise protect me, and I knew that He would give me results. For the next twenty-two years I enjoyed many months of foreign missions ministry every year, until I had ministered in more than sixty-five nations, and I loved every moment of it.

Twenty-Nine

How All This Travel Was Financed

Every year, for more than twenty years, I would be home in Virginia for campmeeting time, and then I would leave the country and be gone for many months of ministry in other countries. It was not unusual for me to be out of the country for six to nine months each year. How these many trips to more than sixty-five countries were financed is an important element of this story.

How is it possible that a girl from a sharecropper family could travel all over the world as I have? First, I am very indebted to the Heflin family for teaching us the life of faith in God. We were taught to obey Him in our daily lives and to trust that He would meet our every need. We were taught to hear His voice and launch forth on what He told us. However ridiculous this seemed in the natural, we were taught to know that He would help us.

Our obedience to God, we were taught, was especially important in our personal giving. Although there are many stories I could share in this regard, one of the early ones stands out in my memory.

I had never been rich, but I had worked most of my adult life and was accustomed to having some pocket money. But after I moved to the camp, I was thrust into the life of faith, and we were expected to believe God for our every need from moment to moment.

During camptime one year, someone placed a hundred-dollar bill into my hand at the close of a service. My, I thought I was rich. I was very excited that my faith was working and God was hearing my prayers. I had been praying and believing Him to help me take an around-the-world trip. I was so excited to have that hundred dollars in my purse.

A hundred-dollar bill, much more common today, was considered very large for that time, and I got that large bill changed into smaller ones so that I could pay my tithe on it and give an offering, and then I put the rest of the money carefully away for safekeeping.

The next day I was walking across the camp-ground when the Lord said to me, "What are you going to do with those eighty-eight dollars?"

I said, "I'm going to keep them for an around-the-world ticket."

"Well, how far do you think you can get on that?" He asked.

How All This Travel Was Financed

I thought about that for a moment before I answered, "Well, not very far, I guess." It was hardly enough to get me to New York to catch an international flight. And before that conversation was over, the Lord had told me to give that money in the offering.

That was not the easiest thing I had ever done. Those eighty-eight dollars meant a lot to me. They represented the increase of my faith and the answer to my prayers. I struggled with the thought of giving that money away so quickly. Still, although it was difficult to do, I managed to obey the Lord.

A week or so later, God spoke to me while the offering was being taken in one of the campmeeting services to give a twenty-dollar bill someone else had given to me. "Put that into the offering too," He urged. I can honestly say that I did not want to give that twenty dollars in the offering. I had personal needs, and who knew when I would receive my next offering. But after struggling with it for a few moments, I decided to go down front and give the money.

While I was standing at the front with others who were giving that day, a lady came up and put something into my hand. Without looking at it, I put it in my pocket. I wanted to concentrate right then on what I was giving to God because I was believing Him for miracles. When I got back to my seat, I looked at what she had given me. It was a check for sixteen hundred dollars, enough for my around-the-world ticket. What a miracle!

The greater miracle was that the woman who had given the money didn't know me and hadn't known my name until the Lord had told it to her. She said she had come all the way from Pennsylvania just to write that check to me. When I found out that God spoke my name to someone, that meant more to me than the check, for I knew that if He could speak my name in Pennsylvania, He could speak my name in India, Nepal, China, Russia or wherever else I happened to be.

What a wonderful miracle of multiplication! I had given my little eighty-eight dollars and my little twenty dollars, but I had given them to the Miracle Worker, and He had done a miracle for me. Now my much larger need was supplied.

This is the way God supplied for me through the years, through miracles in answer to my demonstration of love for Him. As I learned to obey Him, He opened the windows of Heaven and poured His blessings out on me.

Of course, it took other people to be obedient to God to provide those miracles, and everyone who gave in the offering that sent me on each of those trips has a share in the harvest that was reaped. One day in Heaven, those who were saved, those who were filled and those who were healed through my ministry to the nations will personally thank those who gave their money to make it all possible. God keeps good record books, and none of us will lose his or her reward.

Another example comes to mind. When I went to Australia with the two ladies, I was sitting under a tree there one day praying when the Lord spoke to me to give my car away. I had a nice Plymouth that I had bought new, and I had taken good care of it. It still didn't have a lot of miles on it. I loved that car, and God was telling me to give it away. In that moment, however, the Lord put such a joy in my heart at the thought of it that I didn't hesitate. I told Him I was willing to do it.

After I got back to America, however, I got busy in camp activities and conveniently forgot what the Lord had told me. Then one day, while I was in the back room of the dining hall washing dishes, the Lord reminded me of my commitment. Now, instead of feeling joy at the thought of giving the car, I wanted to argue with the Lord. I needed my car, and I carefully explained this to God.

The next three days were misery. The Lord kept telling me to give my car, and I kept telling Him that I already had. After all, I had loaned it to people to go out to their revivals, and I had been generous to loan it to other camp staff members when they needed a car. I reminded God of the day I had loaned it to someone to carry paint, and it had spilled on the floor mat.

I was picking up people for church every Sunday in my car. I was using it for camp business. I had already given it to the Lord. Wasn't that enough?

"That's good," the Lord told me, "but I want you to put the keys in somebody else's hands and not expect them to return the car when they're finished with it." Over and over during those three days, I looked at that car and struggled to obey.

What I wasn't admitting to the Lord or to myself was that the car had some psychological hold on me. It was the last thing I had to show for my twenty-two years of hard work. It seemed to be the only proof that I had not thrown my life away.

This struggle was over more than a car, and the stakes were very high. The Lord had said to me in Australia, "You give Me your car keys, and I'll give you the keys to the nations." In retrospect, it seems foolish that I held onto those two little keys so long. One of them opened the car door and turned on the ignition and the other opened the gas tank, but God was offering me keys that were far more powerful and that opened eternal treasures.

During the services in those three days, God spoke through many people. One prophecy, for instance, said: "Let go, and don't hold on to anything." Every prophecy seemed to be about trusting and obeying God and doing what He said. The more I heard, the tighter I squeezed the keys to my car.

The last straw came late one night when Buddy Makepeace came through the snack bar. He was a big man with a big appetite, and he ordered a hot dog, a hamburger and a cheeseburger. That was light eating for Buddy. He must have weighed three hundred and fifty pounds at the time, and he always said the worst thing he ever had to eat was delicious — and he meant it.

After Buddy got his food, he came over to where I was working and said to me, "Sister Jane, I'm not sure what this means, but God told me to give you this." And with that he handed me a bookmark. It read: "Trust and obey"!

My first reaction was that I wanted to slap him, but then I realized that it wasn't Buddy who was doing this. It was God. He "had my number." I had to stop resisting Him and do what He said. In the end, I could not lose, although giving up my car seemed like a loss to me at the time. The next day I went to Brother Heflin's office, put my car keys in his hand and told him what God had been dealing with me to do.

No sooner had I placed those keys in Pastor Heflin's hands than God spoke to me to do something else, something that nearly knocked me off my feet. He told me He wanted me to pay the fare for a young man to go to Israel.

I protested, "God, if I had been allowed to sell my car instead of giving it away, then I would have enough money to send someone to Israel. Now, I have no money *and* I have no car." My rebellion was short-lived, and I committed to paying the young man's way to Israel. That night something wonderful happened.

The enemy had been berating me all day long, telling me that I had done a very foolish thing. "You will really regret this dumb thing you've done now," he taunted. "One thing's for sure: you won't be driving anymore. How will you get home to see your people every now and then?" There seemed to be many voices coming at me from different directions all at one time, and they were laughing and mocking and accusing.

That night, as we were all worshiping the Lord together, my mind was being torn in many different directions. Then a young lady, Debbie Kendrick, stood up and began to prophesy. She turned to me and prophesied specifically. Through her the Lord said that He was opening the nations, and this opening in the nations would not only be for me to go to them, but He would give me a home in every country where I would always feel at home. Because of that, I would never be lonely.

How All This Travel Was Financed

Many other wonderful things were said that night, and I still keep a copy of that prophecy many years later. As what seemed to be an afterthought, the Lord inserted toward the end of the prophecy that I would not only go to nations, but the time would come when the people of other nations would pay my way to come to them. This was the furthest thing from my imagination at the time.

There was one other portion of the prophecy. The Lord concluded by saying that the day would also come that I would pay for other people to go around the world. Going myself had been difficult enough to believe for. Now He was saying that I would send others. This was more than I could conceive of.

As this word was spoken over my life, a release came with it. Suddenly, light and joy and strength were flowing into my body. I was released from all that heaviness, and I became as light as a feather. I danced all over the front of the Tabernacle and felt like I had wings on my feet and other wings that were bearing up all my weight.

From that day on, I walked in a new release of finances and faith for the nations. As I stepped forth into the nations, God provided my needs — every time. He also helped me to pay the fares of other people going out for Him. And, wonder of wonders, I have had many airline tickets sent to me from other nations, sometimes very poor nations, with invitations to come and minister. This is almost unheard of in our time.

In all of this I learned that God was my Source. If I insisted on holding on to the little I had, I would never gain more in Him. As I released what I had to Him, He was able to multiply it and use it to accomplish great things.

In time, God gave me another car, a better one, and He has done it many times since then. I have given away five cars to date, and if the Lord should speak to me to do it again, I will. The more I give, the more I get.

This explains how a sharecropper's daughter can travel all over the world. We serve a big God who is able to meet our every need. It was good that I was learning these lessons, for much greater challenges lay ahead for me.

Part IV

The Greater Glory

Thirty

Supernatural Oil and "Gold Dust"

Through my friendship with the Phillips family, I was invited to minister in Brazil, and Miriam Phillips was my interpreter. Miriam's parents had been missionaries in Brazil for many years. One of their daughters, Leah, had married a Brazilian pastor, and Miriam had married a pastor here in the States.

After Miriam and her husband came to the camp, they later invited me to speak at a women's meeting in their church in Jacksonville, North Carolina. Miriam sent a tape of the meeting to Leah, and her pastor (who is her brother-in-law) then invited me to come to Brazil for ministry.

I fell in love with the Brazilian people and made several trips there in the years that followed. Something that began there was to lead us all into a greater glory.

It was on my second trip to Brazil that I met Luis and Silvania Machado. Silvania had been healed that year from terminal cancer, and both she and

Luis had received the Lord as their Savior. They were very hungry for more of God, and they came to every service.

One night, I prophesied over all the people in the church, and Luis and Silvania were the very last in line to be prophesied over. As they listened to the good things God was saying to others, Luis joked with his wife that surely there would be nothing good left by the time I got to them. But God had saved the best for last, and when it came their turn, God showed me amazing things that He had for them in the future.

I prayed for them both to receive the baptism of the Holy Spirit, and they received wonderfully. I can still see them sprawled on the floor of that church in the Spirit speaking in tongues. I felt a great love coming forth from them.

Several months later, I was back in Virginia, and I received a phone call from Miriam telling me about something very unusual that was occurring with Silvania. Every day as she prayed, supernatural oil was dripping from her hands.

The next time I went to Brazil, I gave Leah a copy of Mother Heflin's book *God of Miracles*, [1] in which she spoke of seeing the oil phenomenon in some of A.A. Allen's meetings back in the middle of the twentieth century. Leah read the book to the pastor of the church (because he didn't read English).

About a year after the oil first appeared, something

even more unusual began to happen. Now, something that looked like gold dust began coming out of the pores of Silvania's skin during worship services. The pastor collected this "gold dust" and placed it on the sick, and many miracles of healing took place as a result. Later, the oil and the gold sometimes came together.

That fall, Brother Heflin and others accompanied me to Brazil. Among them was Chris Phillips, Miriam's husband. He would serve as our interpreter on the trip. Brother Heflin was especially interested in these signs that were coming forth.

The first night we were there, no mention was made of these phenomena, but the next day when we gathered at the church for prayer, the pastor said to Brother Heflin, "Come; I want to show you something." He showed us two buckets of oil and many smaller containers full of oil and said that it had all dripped from Silvania's hands during her times of prayer.

He opened one container and let us smell it. It had a very unique, sweet scent, like nothing that any of us had ever smelled before. It was wonderful. Then he told us the entire story, from beginning to end, how it had started and the progression of events.

Brother Heflin said to me later, "If you see Silvania when the oil is on her hands, tell her to come and lay her hands on my bald head." The next day, as we were praying, Silvania came into the service. There was oil dripping from her hands, and you could see drops of it on the floor where she had walked. Before the morning was over, she prayed for all of us.

Brother Heflin wanted to take back some photos of the gold. It was not happening then in the same abundance it would later. Later, it would pour from her scalp in great abundance. Then, it was appearing in scattered patches on her face and neck. Still, it was just as miraculous and just as anointed.

I told a brother who was taking pictures for Brother Heflin not to use up all of the film early in the service because I knew the gold would come in greater abundance later. But he got so excited when he saw miracles taking place that he used up all his film and was not able to get the very best photos. Nevertheless, Brother Heflin was thrilled to see these unusual phenomena.

The next time I was in Brazil for meetings, the more abundant manifestation of this miracle had already begun, and Miriam had told me about it. I made a point of examining Silvania carefully every night to make sure that what was happening was real. I examined her hair, and I examined her hands, and was satisfied that she had nothing hidden. Then I would watch her as the miracle came. At some point in the service, she would indicate to the pastor that the gold had come, and then it would pour forth from her hair. It happened like that every single night for fourteen nights.

The pastor had put together a video of this occurrence from some of their meetings, and he graciously allowed me to take a copy of the video home to Virginia with me that Christmastime.

I gave Sister Ruth a little bottle with some of the oil in it and one with some of the "gold dust." I told her about the video and asked her if she would like for me to show it to others in the camp. She had me show it one night after the services, and when she saw it, she knew immediately that this great sign was from God. She wept for joy at the sight of it. After that, she had me show the video every week so that others could see it.

For a while, I showed it every Saturday afternoon and sometimes on Sunday too, depending on how many new people there were in the service who wanted to see it. Some wanted to see it over and over again. This was interesting, because the entire video was in Portuguese, and most of us couldn't understand anything that was being said. We knew a miracle when we saw it, and it made us hungry for more of God's power.

Then, suddenly, in February of that year, during our 1998 Winter Campmeeting, this same miracle began to happen in our services too. Sister Ruth had a little "gold dust" on her, it came on me, and several others got it on them. It wasn't much at first, but we got excited every time it came, we showed it to others, and many were blessed by it.

That summer Silvania came and spoke for the first time in our Summer Campmeeting, and her miracle was seen live for the first time here in this country. Leah and Miriam and the pastor's wife from Brazil and others came too, and Miriam served as Silvania's interpreter. The miracle of the "gold dust" so stirred people that they began to seek God as never before. From then on, the "gold dust" rained down on all of us in our campmeeting services, even when Silvania wasn't there.

After camp was over, this miracle happened in all the meetings I had outside the camp, and the same thing happened with Sister Ruth, both here and abroad. She prayed for many other people, and it happened to them. Then they prayed for others, and it happened to them too.

The phenomenon increased so rapidly and happened in so many places that Sister Ruth eventually wrote her book *Golden Glory*, [2] documenting what was happening. The book contains testimonies of people from all over the world who had experienced the same thing or something very similar.

Since that time, Silvania has come several times each year to speak for us in the camp in Ashland,

and this miracle continues to manifest itself each time she comes. As of now, I have been with her in thirty-seven different services (here and in Brazil), and the "gold dust" has not failed to come even one time.

The same is true of the oil. It stopped for three days once, and Silvania realized that it was because she was angry with someone. She repented of her anger, and the oil began to flow again. Since then, it has not ceased — even for a single day.

It has been a great privilege to be part of what God is doing in Silvania's life. Now she is ministering all over the world, and God is using her to bring healing to many people with cancer and to many people with broken homes. The love that I felt radiating from her when I first met her in Brazil has now been experienced by many thousands of people. Everyone comments on it.

These manifestations of "gold dust" and supernatural oil have spread to believers all over the world, and God is being glorified in a new way in our midst. This has caused us to have an expectancy for greater signs and wonders to come.

1. Heflin, Edith Ward, *God of Miracles*, Destiny Image Publishers (Shippensburg, Pennsylvania: 1991).
2. Heflin, Ruth Ward, *Golden Glory*, McDougal Publishing (Hagerstown, Maryland: 1999).

Thirty-One

The Passing of the Torch

After we finished our prayer time at the camp on the morning of December 26, 1997, I got ready to leave. With Debbie Slayton, one of our faithful camp workers, I would be visiting a funeral home in Westpoint, Virginia, because the grandmother of one of our camp ladies had died. Then I would be spending the night in Williamsburg with Debbie's mother and flying out of the Williamsburg/Newport News Airport the next day for Jacksonville, Florida, to visit my brother William and his family.

I passed Brother Heflin as he was on the way to his office, and told him I was leaving for the funeral home. "Wait a minute," he said, and he went to his car and pulled out a package he had there. It was a beautiful piece of carved soapstone from China, and he was offering it as a gift for my brother William and for Jimmie Lee, his wife. This was very typical of Brother Heflin. He had always been a very generous person.

Christmas had always been a wonderful time at the camp, and we had all enjoyed yet another joyful season together. Soon, however, our lives were to be seriously disrupted.

For some reason, Debbie and I spoke between ourselves on the way about what would become of the camp ministry if something ever happened to Brother Heflin. We knew that he had not been feeling well recently, but we could not imagine that his departure was imminent. *Who could ever replace him?* we wondered together. We couldn't think of anyone. He was a unique personality, and everyone agreed that he was larger than life.

After his father's death in 1972, his mother had taken on some of the burden of the local church in Richmond, but Wallace, Jr., had become the bearer of the torch for the camp and foreign missions. Now his mother was quite elderly, and he had been carrying the full burden of the ministry for many years.

It was a huge vision, and it carried with it a huge burden of responsibility. The ministry had begun with one short summer campmeeting and a few small churches. Now there were two annual campmeetings — summer and winter — and there were many special conventions being conducted at camp. There were the trips abroad, all the various missionary activities, the tent meetings and special meetings in cities around America and also the radio and television programs and the books that were being published. What could we ever do without Brother Heflin? We couldn't imagine.

Jimmie Lee picked me up at the airport in Jacksonville that afternoon, and when William came home from work that evening we all went out to eat together. We spent a lovely evening together, and late that night I had just gone to bed when the phone rang. When I heard Jimmie Lee say, "Yes, she's here," I knew that something was wrong. It was after midnight, and no one would be calling me at that time of the night otherwise.

It was Debbie Slayton, and I couldn't believe what she was telling me. Brother Heflin had suffered a massive heart attack coming home from a visit to the same funeral home, and he had never recovered consciousness. He was gone.

The moment was surreal. I was sure that what she was saying could not possibly be true, but I was also sure that she would not call me if something had not happened.

"It can't be!" I insisted.

"But it is!" she answered.

"It just can't be," I said.

"But it is," she told me. "It's the truth. He's gone."

The news was particularly devastating to me because of the timing. We had lost our mother in

February of that year, and now I had lost my spiritual father and mentor as well.

Soon after Debbie and I hung up, I began to make arrangements to fly back to camp the next day, but even as I did, my mind was in a turmoil.

"Why?" my mind shouted. "Why would this happen?" I was afraid to voice the question to God. He always did things well, but His reasons were surely hidden to me this time. I couldn't imagine why this would happen. We expected Brother Heflin to outlive us all.

My mind rushed back over the past few weeks. Brother Heflin and I had traveled with that small group of people to Brazil, and there we had witnessed the amazing things of which I spoke in the last chapter. Many Brazilians had been healed and set free as he laid his hands on them and prayed. He had insisted that I minister every other night, but I thought this was just his kind way of giving me an opportunity. I never dreamed that he was getting us ready for the days ahead — when he would no longer be with us.

Because there had been just a few of us in the team, I had been able to speak more with him in a few days than I had over many years, and we had talked of many things concerning the future of the camp. He had been excited about the future and did not seem to be making plans to leave us. He had a lot to live for. Things were going very well for him and his ministry worldwide.

He *had* seemed to have had a very bad cold during those days, but none of us had considered it to be anything life-threatening. This was a man who didn't let anything keep him down, and yet now he was gone. He was dead. What would happen to the camp ministry? What would happen to all of us?

Because it involved a death, the airlines gave me no problem about changing my ticket, but I then encountered a series of flight delays and changes throughout the day. Atlanta was fogged in, so my flight was late leaving for there. Then, when I did get into Atlanta, I couldn't get out. In the end, I was not able to fly into Richmond at all. I had to be rerouted to Dulles Airport near Washington, D.C., and I had to call for someone to pick me up there. It took me sixteen hours to get home.

During those hours getting back to camp, I was not feeling very good about what I would find once I got there. Who would be there? What changes faced us all in the days ahead? Was there anyone who could pick up the pieces and keep us moving forward? The camp team was made up of people of such distinct personalities. Brother Heflin had been strong enough to pull us all together, but could we all work well together in his absence? I wasn't sure that we could.

As I contemplated all of this, a song began to work its way into my spirit: "I will arise and go forth in the name of the Lord of Hosts, for He has conquered every foe by His name, by His name." I wept as those words went over and over in my spirit, and I began to feel strength coming into my mind, my spirit and my body.

What I would face when I got back I still wasn't sure, but I knew that every foe had been conquered — even death. The death of our leader would not be allowed to bring a halt to the great ministry of the camp.

And the other foe — the fear of what our continued living might mean — was conquered during those hours as well. My mind still couldn't comprehend how we could go forward without Brother Heflin, but my spirit was at peace about the prospect.

Over the next few days, thousands of people came from around this country and the world to pay their respects to a great man who had touched so many lives. During the viewing, he was kept in the camp for several days, and a steady stream of mourners moved by his casket. Then he was moved to the Richmond church one night, and the church was filled as it never had been filled before. Then one of the largest auditoriums in Richmond had to be rented to accommodate the crowd for the actual funeral.

As men and women stood at his casket during those days, they remembered what they had been and what they were now, and they gave thanks to God for Wallace Heflin's part in bringing about this great change. It was a very touching time and a very challenging time. Somehow we had to carry forward his vision. But how was that possible?

Letters, faxes, e-mails and cables poured in from around the world during those days. Wallace Heflin had touched rich and poor alike. Most of the expressions of gratitude for his life and what it meant to so many included a prayer that his vision would go forward. People were praying for us that we could carry on. And surely we must — somehow.

Although we had come to love and appreciate Brother Heflin through the years, we somehow came to understand there beside his casket what a very great man he had been and how blessed we had been to be part of his life. We had traveled with him to many nations, and he had taught us to do the work as well. We had stood with him in tent meetings, campmeetings and conventions at home and abroad and seen tens of thousands of lives changed, and he had allowed us to be part of it. What a privilege! We were grateful to God.

We had known that he was someone very special,

and yet we had not known the depths of that truth. It was a moving experience to hear it from everyone else. He had been a pastor, a friend and a father to so many. He had loved to preach, but he was also the same in his office or out working somewhere on the campground. Anywhere he was, when he met people in need, he could reach in and get a word from the Lord for them and believe God for a miracle for their lives.

He had a wonderful ability as an encourager. When any of us sat down with him and began to unburden ourselves, we knew before we left him that everything would work out for the good, that God was in control. Who could possibly fill such large shoes?

It came as a profound relief to all of us — a relief beyond words — when, during the funeral, God began to speak to Sister Ruth to leave Jerusalem and come back home to take charge of the ministry. Two people were especially used to convey to her this message: Dr. Gwen R. Shaw and Dr. William A. Ward.

We all knew how much Sister Ruth loved Jerusalem, and because of that we had not considered for a moment that she would be willing to leave what had become her home to come back to Virginia permanently. As it turned out, God had been speaking to her for some time about returning to America.

She just hadn't been sure of the timing, and she had no idea that it would involve the death of her brother.

Suddenly, everything was turned around, and our despair turned to rejoicing. Ruth Ward Heflin had known the Lord long before her brother was saved. She had been a missionary already when he was still running from God. She encouraged him in his younger years of ministry, and he often looked to her for guidance. Surely the camp ministry would enjoy a great future under the capable leadership of this gifted woman!

Thirty-Two

To New Heights of Glory

I would not want to suggest that it was an easy transition from the leadership of Wallace Heflin, Jr., to that of his sister. We were all accustomed to his style of leadership, and she had a totally different style. This created a lot of tension in the camp family, and we lost some of our team members in the transition.

But this was nothing new. There had always been a large turnover of volunteers in the camp. Camp life was never easy, and it demanded a special dedication. It was clearly not for everyone. In the coming months and years, however, the camp ministries not only continued — they exploded.

Part of the difficulty in that transition period was a new emphasis the Lord gave Sister Ruth on revival in America. The entire camp family had been oriented through the years to have a burden for the nations, and she herself had played a great role in developing that burden in us. She lived out that vision and visited every nation on the face of the earth for the sake of the Gospel. Now, however, she began to feel that it was time for revival in America and that we should stay home for a while and help our own people move into revival.

It would be necessary to understand how strong our love for the nations was to know why this caused so much friction among the staff members. For some, it was devastating.

I understood what everyone was feeling, but at the same time, I couldn't feel that we had anything to complain about. God knew that we desperately needed leadership, and He had supplied it for us. Sister Ruth was ushering us into an entirely new realm of glory than we had been accustomed to. I responded by canceling some of the foreign meetings I had scheduled for that year. If God was doing something, I wanted to be a part of it. America deserved her time of revival.

Almost immediately, things began to happen at the campground on a larger scale and with more ease than ever before. Improvements we had wanted to make to the camp facility for years were suddenly made, and it happened very easily and quickly and without the camp having to go into debt to do it.

Suddenly, the camp had two new vans, and they were paid for. Suddenly, there were new parking lots, and they were paid for. Suddenly, the entrance road was widened, and that construction was paid for.

The camp had long been known for its worship, but now that was deepened. Sister Ruth encouraged us to go deeper in worship, to see Jesus and touch Him and experience Him. People from every branch of Christianity began to be drawn to Ashland to experience this new depth of worship and to touch Heaven.

As the great river of God began to be poured forth in many parts of the land, we also were awash in its power. Sister Ruth taught us how to stand in the river of God and how to flow with that river. She encouraged us to lose our fear of the river's currents, and be swept away with it — wherever it happened to be taking us at the moment.

This was a glorious experience. In every service we were moving into new and different waters. We were moving from glory to glory, from vision to vision, and from one heavenly touch to another.

Because of her years spent overseas, Sister Ruth was relatively unknown around America. Now, because of her book *Glory*, [1] and because she was invited to some very prominent meetings, her fame suddenly skyrocketed, and she was in great demand around the country.

She was speaking in Pensacola at the revival there. She was invited by Pastor Benny Hinn to his crusades. Many times he would have her stand up before everyone, and then he would tell how she had prophesied to him before he had begun his ministry, telling him that all of the things he was currently experiencing would happen. She prophesied to many more of America's spiritual leaders at the Revivalfest at CBN in Virginia Beach, Virginia. Before long, she had a thousand invitations, many more than she could possibly fill, and she was flying off here and there around the country to minister.

That next summer, the camp was more crowded than it had ever been before. As the summer was coming to an end, Sister Ruth said that the Lord had spoken to her to continue having weekend revival meetings. By now, she had written her second book, *Revival Glory,* [2] and she was calling these meetings Revival Glory Meetings. They were conducted in the camp every Friday night, Saturday morning and Saturday evening. On Sunday morning we all went into the Richmond church, and then we were back at the camp for the evening service.

Usually, Sister Ruth would fly out again late Sunday night or early on Monday to some other crusade. Then she would come back to Virginia that following Friday for the weekend meetings again. Two things were happening through all of this: God was using Sister Ruth in revival around America, and He was getting some of the rest of us ready for the future when she would no longer be with us.

Some months after she returned from Jerusalem, Sister Ruth began to give me added responsibilities. Among other things, she asked me to sit beside her during services so that I could carry out her desires in each service. That first summer, she allotted one week for me as one of the main campmeeting speakers, and she did the same thing the following year. During that special week, I was relieved of all other camp duties so that I could concentrate on the ministry that would be required of me.

That was a big step for me — and for all of us. None of the camp staff members had ever served as special speakers. Although we spoke occasionally, the main speaker slots were usually reserved for outside speakers. Outsiders brought with them a fresh word from God. Now, it was a great challenge for me to do what needed to be done, and I had to press in to God as never before. People were depending on me.

Before the 1999 campmeeting season started, Sister Ruth let me know that my role had changed — drastically. I would not have time to fulfill other duties, and neither would I be able to speak one week. My principal duty would be directing the evening services.

The two-services-a-day format that we had adopted for the weekend revival meetings was also adopted for all of our campmeetings. Through the years, the services had become longer and longer as the people moved into greater depths of worship and as they spent more time basking in the Lord's presence, and the services had begun bumping into each other and overlapping. Having just two services a day allowed us to worship without having to worry about the time. We could stay as long as we wanted in the Lord's presence.

This eliminated the afternoon service I had been responsible for over the past ten years, but I had plenty of other responsibilities. Although someone else would take charge of the morning services, I had to make sure that all the services went well.

It was a very exciting time for all of us. People from around the country and from many other nations began to make their way to Ashland for revival. Many of these came because they had read the books, and the books kept coming: *River Glory*, [3] *Golden Glory*, [4] *Unifying Glory*, [5] *Harvest Glory* [6] and *Revelation Glory*. [7] All of these came forth in just a few years' time in that wonderful flow of revival.

But Sister Ruth's time with us was also to be cut short, although, again, we had not foreseen it. There is an old saying that you can't see the forest for the trees, and I think that was the case with having Ruth Ward Heflin among us. We sat under her ministry and we heard her words. We experienced with her the things so many thousands of others have read about and marveled at, but I'm sure we did not appreciate the depths of the woman whom God had placed among us.

Imagine! She had traveled to every known nation in the world. She had met and ministered to great world leaders prophetically. In all of her travels, she had been moved solely by the word of the Lord, nothing else. People from all nations had come to Jerusalem and to Ashland to receive her wisdom. We loved her and respected her, but we surely did not fully appreciate her and the impact she had made on her time.

As we look back now, there are many things we can point to and say that she taught us, but probably the greatest is the ease she brought in the glory. That is what sustained us after she suddenly took flight and left us on September 15, 2000.

We were a little better prepared for Ruth Ward Heflin's death than we had been for her brother's. In the summer of 1999, she had been in an automobile accident late one night as she was on her way north to a meeting near Philadelphia. As a result, one of her ankles was broken, and she was confined somewhat over the next six months as the bone healed and she learned to use her leg again. In the meantime, she insisted on coming to the services in a wheelchair, and a special ramp was constructed so that she could come onto the platform.

The following spring, just before Easter, we learned that Sister Ruth had breast cancer and would be undergoing surgery. She was at peace with this turn of events. Her only concern was not to become a hindrance to the revival, and every decision she made in the days ahead was based on that consideration. She wanted only the best for all of us.

During the brief months of sickness that followed this until her death, Sister Ruth was never sad. She was never discouraged. She was never downhearted. She had a great expectancy for the future.

If we had taken closer notice, we might have understood what was happening. She had begun to speak more of heavenly things, especially of seeing Jesus. The theme she selected for the 2000 Summer Campmeeting was "Face to Face." Later, we would realize that this had been prophetic. She was approaching her appointment with destiny. At the moment, however, we could only enjoy experiencing the glory of His presence in our own way.

The opening service of Summer Campmeeting 2000 was very moving. She had been recovering her strength little by little since the surgery, and she was determined to come into the services a little each night, and to continue recovering strength until she was completely well again. That night, as she came onto the platform in her wheelchair, there were five prominent men, all evangelists in great demand, who had canceled their own meetings and come to stand behind her and believe with her for healing. She preached that night, and they stood behind her as she ministered. It was wonderful.

She stayed through every service all that week. She went on to speak a number of times that summer, usually on Sunday mornings, and her final messages were especially powerful.

Her fight to restore her health proved to be an uphill battle. During the second week of camp, she broke her pelvis, just by moving, and then she broke several ribs. From that time on she was in severe pain.

She had taught us to stand in the glory, to reach into the glory and pull down what the people needed, and we continued to do this in her absence, all the while believing that she would fully recover. Now she was gone, and again we had some very big shoes to fill. Could it be possible that I had been chosen to fill those shoes? How could I possibly fulfill such a great responsibility?

1. Heflin, Ruth Ward, *Glory*, McDougal Publishing (Hagerstown, Maryland: 1996).
2. Heflin, Ruth Ward, *Revival Glory*, McDougal Publishing (Hagerstown, Maryland: 1998).

3. Heflin, Ruth Ward, *River Glory*, McDougal Publishing (Hagerstown, Maryland: 1999).
4. Heflin, Ruth Ward, *Golden Glory*, McDougal Publishing (Hagerstown, Maryland: 2000).
5. Heflin, Ruth Ward, *Unifying Glory,* McDougal Publishing (Hagerstown, Maryland: 2000).
6. Heflin, Ruth Ward, *Harvest Glory*, McDougal Publishing (Hagerstown, Maryland: 2000).
7. Heflin, Ruth Ward, *Revelation Glory,* McDougal Publishing (Hagerstown, Maryland: 2001).

Thirty-Three

Filling Gigantic Shoes

Looking back now, I think that Brother Heflin knew that his time was approaching. Why he didn't tell us I'm not sure. But he had certainly poured his heart into us through the years, getting us ready to carry on in his stead. I'm happy for him, and I know that he wouldn't want to come back. But we miss him a lot.

Sister Ruth also didn't tell us in so many words. Her accident and her sickness prepared us better for what happened, but still her passing was a shock to all of us. We somehow thought she would live forever. She did say to me several times, "If something happens to me, carry on," and I suppose that was enough.

Neither of them spoke to us of death, but rather of life. They were planning their next strategies for the Kingdom when God took them.

The last time that I spoke with Sister Ruth on the campground, she was preparing to go to the hospital.

I ran over to her home to ask her about the theme for the upcoming conventions. Although it was about ten o'clock at night, she didn't mind my intrusion at all into her moment of physical suffering.

I said to her, "We haven't talked yet about our banner, and about what our theme will be for the Ladies' Convention and the Men's Convention."

"No," she said, "we didn't talk about that, did we?"

I said, "No, Ma'am, we didn't."

She said, "We must talk about that."

She closed her eyes for a moment, and then she opened them again. For those of us who knew her well, it was a typical way she had of searching the Spirit and letting God drop something into her heart. She often heard from Heaven in this way. When she opened her eyes, she would have the word she was looking for.

She closed her eyes for another moment and then opened them again, and she said, "The Revealed Glory."

But she wasn't satisfied with this theme. She closed her eyes again, saying, "No! No!" And when she opened them this time, she had the theme we were looking for. "The Days of Revealed Glory," she told me with a smile, and that became our theme for the coming months.

I marveled at this. She was leaving for the hospital

within the next thirty minutes, and yet her thoughts were still on our receiving revealed glory.

I had intended to go back to the Tabernacle, but she asked me to accompany her to the hospital. As someone was driving her away from the place she had so loved, she was still pondering what God would do for us in the Ladies' Convention and in the Men's Convention. Until very recently she had been working with some of the men on the plans for the new worship center across the road. She was still talking about the nations coming there to be blessed. Her vision was still fresh and vibrant.

The next time she returned to the camp, it would be in a casket, but the vision she left us could not be allowed to die. The faith she instilled in us could not be allowed to perish. We were determined to rise up and go after the vision left to us and to see the glory of God revealed in a way we had not yet known it or seen it.

When the news came from the hospital that she was gone, I gathered all of our camp people together in the dining hall. I told them what I knew and comforted and strengthened them. I was sure that we would go forward, I told them — somehow. God was not dead. He was with us.

They were brave words, but when I reached the privacy of my own house, I did something that I had rarely done in my entire life, even as a child.

I stomped my feet and said to God, "How could You do this to me? I didn't ask for this."

Two weeks before that, Brother McDougal, who is a member of our trustee board at the camp and a close friend of the Heflins for longer than I had known them, as well as their publisher (and now mine), had been about to leave for home one day after visiting Sister Ruth to work with her on her latest book, *Revelation Glory.* Although she was very weak, she had been able to read through the manuscript and was satisfied that it was as she wanted it. He saw me outside the dining hall, drove over and put his car window down. "I'm praying for you," he said. "One day very soon a very heavy weight will fall on your shoulders."

"That thought terrifies me," I told him, hoping that he was wrong. But now that it had happened, it was fully as terrifying as I had anticipated. "You can't do this to me!" I shouted at God.

As I look back on it now, I realize how foolish this was. I had come to the camp nearly twenty-five years before, believing God to send me to the nations. What I had gotten at first was washing dishes, mixing mortar, digging ditches, teaching others to use the chain saw, splitting wood, cleaning toilets, installing roofing and learning carpentry chores like installing flooring and siding. I had driven the trash truck for several years. I had done the shopping.

I had unloaded tractor-trailer loads of food for the camp kitchen, and I had done many other menial tasks. But as I had been doing these things, God had been preparing me for the future.

Even when I had begun to go out to the nations and I would come back to camp, I was returned to menial tasks. Overseas, I would have wonderful meetings with great miracles and much fruit, and then I would come back and take charge of the dish room and the snack bar, and I would rake leaves and paint.

Most of us who lived at camp through the years had relatively few opportunities to minister in camp itself. There were always too many of us, and, as I said, preference was given to outsiders who would come in with a fresh word. For many years, in any given summer, I may have been able to speak two or three times, but not more than that. Each year, when camp was over, I would take another trip overseas, then come back and return to the dish room and the snack bar once again.

When I was put in charge of the afternoon service, this had seemed like a big step up. I soon found that it required even greater sacrifice. I had to be in every afternoon service because I was in charge of seeing that we had someone to lead the worship and that the offering was taken, and then I introduced the afternoon speaker. Even then, my duties were not finished. I had to stay until the speaker that day had finished, whatever time that happened to be (and sometimes it was as late as seven that evening or even later). Then I was expected to be back in the Tabernacle that night at eight for the main service.

This responsibility was not just for one day or one week, but it went on day after day for ten and a half weeks of summer camp for ten years straight. Early on, I noticed that if I wasn't careful, doing such services every day for ten and a half weeks could become ordinary, and it would have been easy to do what was expected of me and no more. I was determined to reach into God every day and to have something fresh for the people.

I realized very early in my camp experience that if I did only what was expected of me, I was missing it. I am so thankful that the Heflin family expected a lot from us. Their expectations caused us to stretch ourselves and to believe for greater things. If I had gone through the paces and my heart hadn't been in it, I would not have received anything. During those ten years of leading the afternoon service, I asked God to help me so that in every service I would be alert and that I would be an encourager and a strength to the person who was ministering that day. And God had done wonderful things in my life because of it.

The enemy had always been there to tell me that

I wasn't getting enough opportunities to speak, that I wasn't getting enough opportunities to lead the really important services, and that I had no future in the camp ministry. We all fought these battles, and they didn't get any easier as time went on. He had tried to make us feel left out, forgotten and neglected. But in all of this time, God had been developing something in me. He had been bringing forth a purity and strength that could cause me to do greater things for Him.

He had an appointed day in which all of this would be revealed, and that day had come. Why should I complain to Him now? Yes, it was scary to try to fill such gigantic shoes. Yes, it was scary to take on such a large responsibility, but just as He had been with me every step of the way, helping me to overcome test after test, I was sure that He would be with me now. I had not gotten this far in my own strength, and I would not try to go forward in my own strength. But He was with me. Every time I had said, "Okay, Lord, You do it," He had done it, and I knew that He would not fail me now.

Sometimes when I look back and I think about Brother Wallace Heflin and his leadership and of Sister Ruth and her leadership, I want to cry. At other times, I want to rejoice. They are gone and have left us here still running the race. Sometimes that makes me feel like I could conquer the whole world, but at other moments I want to run as fast as I can and leave all of my new responsibilities behind.

"Who am I?" I have often asked God. "Just a sharecropper's daughter thrust into this big world of responsibility." Then I look up and see His face again, and I know that the race is worth the prize and that seeing Him *High and Lifted Up* will sustain me.

Thirty-Four

Continuing the Legacy

What is this legacy that has been left to us? We must understand it if we are to carry it forward. Some spiritual giants have gone before us, and we are now privileged to walk in their footsteps and to carry forward their vision. We have some gigantic shoes to fill.

The Calvary Pentecostal Church and Campground, of which I am now the pastor and director, was founded by Rev. and Mrs. Wallace Heflin, Sr. I never knew Brother Heflin, Sr., because he died a few years before I came to the camp. I have read and heard many things about him. The thing we most often hear and read is that he was a great man of faith, who reached out, not only to the individuals and towns around him but also to the world.

There are many monuments to this man's faith, including the camp itself. He was a man so compelled to action that he was always looking for a good lot to set up his tent and preach in any given community. Because of that, he established small congregations in many Virginia communities. These congregations, many of which still exist today, speak for his steadfastness and dedication. There are also many men and women in the ministry who were challenged by his life.

Reverend Edith Ward Heflin, his wife, was the daughter of ministers and was a preacher before her husband became a preacher. She was born in Los Angeles, where her parents had gone to be part of the great Azusa Street Revival of the early part of the past century.

I am eternally grateful to God for this holy woman, for her love and patience and for her constant challenge to spiritual excellence. She made us to know God's wonderful ways and taught us that we could know *Him*. She taught us that we could have visions, that we could prophesy, that we could go to the nations. Then, she stood behind us in prayer and fasting and sent us on our way to do it. She must have been up a few nights wondering how we were doing and if we were exalting the name of Jesus as we should and praying for us.

These two giants of the faith deposited their vision in their children, Betty, Wallace, Jr., and Ruth Ward Heflin. Betty died quite young and left four small children for Mother Heflin to raise, and I have already spoken of the spiritual giants, Wallace, Jr., and Ruth, and of their impact upon all of our lives.

Continuing the Legacy

There is another giant who no longer walks among us whom I must also mention more in detail. He is Dr. William A. Ward. (Dr. Ward was Mother Heflin's brother.) He preached for more than sixty years before God took him home in July of 1999. He was the author of many books and is widely quoted, but to us he was the man who spoke faith every time he opened his mouth. For many years, he deposited faith into us and challenged us to do great things for God.

There are many wonderful stories that serve as examples of his unique anointing, but the one I love most was about the leper colony in the Bahamas. He took a month's leave from the church he was pastoring in Tulsa, Oklahoma, and went to the Bahamas for tent revivals. In a single service there, he prayed for more than two hundred blind people, and most of them were healed. When this happened, he was invited to a local leper colony.

The authorities of the colony were very strict and would not allow him to touch any of the lepers. In fact, when they brought out fifty-six lepers and lined them up to receive prayer, they drew a line and made him stand back fifty feet from them. He went down that line praying for each of the fifty-six lepers individually, and because he felt that God was indeed moving, he declared them all to be healed.

Toward the end of his prayer, he realized that not

every leper had come out (some were too ill), and he said, "For all those lepers inside the building who are too sick to come out ... I pronounce them healed also."

The law required that a doctor visit the patients every two weeks for an entire year before he could declare them healed. A missionary who was one of Dr. Ward's friends went with the doctor on every visit to the colony and later reported that every single one of those lepers had been healed. This included not only the fifty-six who had lined up outside for prayer, but those who had been inside too. In all, one hundred lepers were healed, and the facility was permanently closed. Later, two of those men who had been healed contacted Dr. Ward and told him that they were now ministers in the Assemblies of God. Thank God for such a man as William A. Ward.

When I came to Ashland in the mid-1970s, the ministry of the camp was still relatively small, but faith was already large. God was speaking to us of the coming of the nations. Some of us wondered if that could happen, but it surely has. In our campmeetings and conventions now, we often have up to forty nations represented at any one time, and the ministry is making an impact on the world. This all began as a vision in the heart of a man and woman of faith. It was passed on to their children, and now it has been left to us. What a privilege this is!

Continuing the Legacy

So, what is our legacy? It is a legacy of faith in God, a legacy of liberty in the Holy Spirit, a legacy of hope for the world, a legacy of experiencing the glory and taking it to men and women everywhere.

One thing had bothered me about our ministry in recent years. I loved going to the nations, and standing still hadn't been easy for me. I had so many nations in my heart that, although I did love my own country, not being able to go out as I had for many years was not a pleasant thing for me.

I spoke with Sister Ruth about this, and she assured me that she had not lost her vision for the nations. The emphasis on America was a matter of timing, she said. She had felt that she must play a major role in it, and she had. We would indeed continue our outreach to the nations.

One night before Summer Campmeeting 2000 began, she gave a prophetic word about the nations, and I knew that our time of staying home was at an end. She said nothing more about it, but the weeping that had come when she gave that word convinced me. Soon after that, we sent missionaries from the camp again as we had in the previous years.

And so the vision goes forward. Can we possibly fill such gigantic shoes? I am convinced that we can — if we will continue to look to Him who is *High and Lifted Up.* When I took my own first steps of faith, I didn't know what I would do or how I would do it.

But my lack of knowledge and experience proved to be a blessing, causing me to cry out to God, and He was there to help me. That same cry, coming forth from our hearts today and tomorrow, will enable us to answer the current challenge.

I have experienced that anytime we get to the place that we think we know everything, it becomes difficult for us to hear the voice of the Lord. If we always know exactly where we are going and exactly what we will say and do when we get there, we are not leaving much room for God to work. In those early days, I didn't know anybody, but He knew everybody. I didn't know the hearts of the people, but He knew them. I didn't know what the people needed, but He knew. Now, we must lean heavily upon the Lord in this new time in our lives. Surely He will not fail us.

Nearly a full year has gone by since the day I stood in Sister Ruth's funeral and heard the applause of those people, welcoming me as their new pastor and as the new director of this great ministry. We are currently moving forward with all of the camp activities — the campmeetings, the conventions and the outreaches. Our Winter Campmeeting 2001 was blessed, our spring conventions have been packed out and full of life, and we are moving forward with the building of the two-thousand-seat Ruth Ward Heflin Memorial Worship Center.

Land has been purchased for this purpose, and substantial sums of money have already been raised. We are about halfway to our goal. I remember praying all night in India when I needed five hundred and thirty-eight dollars. Now we are believing for millions. Groundbreaking is scheduled to take place for the new building soon. When this building is completed, it will seriously increase our capacity to reach out to our community and the world.

I was reminded recently of a vision I had very shortly after I came to the camp in 1977. In the vision, the Lord took me by the hand and led me around the campground, and as He did, He pointed out the various buildings that existed at the time and reminded me of the sacrifice that had gone into each one of them. "If you will enter into this vision," He said to me, "and become a part of what they are doing here, I will cause others to enter into your vision. And they will be a strength to you in carrying out your vision." It took me all these years to realize the greatness of what God said to me that day. Now, I am so glad that I got under the vision of the founders and directors of this ministry. And I am extremely grateful for all of those who are now helping me to move forward with the vision the Lord has given me for the future.

Epilogue

A Visit Back Home

Once, when I went home to North Carolina for a visit, I drove out to see the old farm place where we grew up. The house was gone, but the well house was still standing and some of the old fruit trees. The pine thicket had been removed, and someone had joined the two big fields into one.

I drove by the old mill where we had taken our corn and wheat to be ground. Much of the mill was fallen down, but enough was still standing that I could visualize it as it had been in my childhood. Those ruins probably wouldn't mean much to other people, but they meant a lot to me that day. I could see us children gathered around the machines watching them grind our corn into meal. It all brought back a lot of good memories.

But soon the moment passed. It's another day and another time, and thank God that we don't have to live on memories. Even visions have to be renewed. Yesterday's visions are not good enough for today, and we cannot live off of the past. God has bright tomorrows for each of us.

The visions I experienced first in 1975 were wonderful, and I can still see them today and still get excited about them. The joy that accompanied those visions was life-changing, and I can still experience that joy now every time I think about them. But this is a new millennium, a far different time, and we need new visions for a new generation and a new time on God's calendar.

I have been particularly blessed in that the Lord has given me so many visions of Himself. I am convinced that He wants to do this for each of us. He wants to show us many things about Himself. For instance, He wants us to understand His heart for the lost. He wants to catch each of us up into a new place in the heavens and show us things we have not yet known. He wants to give us all a glimpse of Himself *High and Lifted Up.*

GLORY

by
Ruth Ward Heflin

What is Glory?

- *It is the realm of eternity.*
- *It is the revelation of the presence of God.*
- *He is the glory! As air is the atmosphere of the Earth, so glory is the atmosphere of Heaven.*

Praise ... until the spirit of worship comes. Worship ... until the glory comes. Then ... stand in the glory. If you can capture the basic principles of praise, worship and glory that are outlined in this book — so simple that we often miss them — you can have anything else you want in God.

ISBN 1-884369-00-6 $10.00

Ask for it at your favorite bookstore or from:

Calvary Books
11352 Heflin Lane
Ashland, VA 23005
(804) 798-7756
www.revivalglory2.org

REVIVAL GLORY
by Ruth Ward Heflin

What is Revival Glory?

- *It is standing in the cloud and ministering directly from the cloud of God's glory unto the people.*
- *It is seeing into the eternal realm and declaring what you are seeing.*
- *It is gathering in the harvest, using only the tools of the Spirit.*
- *It is, ultimately, the revelation of Jesus Christ.*

One cannot have revival without the glory or the glory without having revival.

ISBN 1-884369-80-4 $13.00

RIVER GLORY
by Ruth Ward Heflin

What is River Glory?

Through the analogy of the river, God has given us a whole new consciousness of His Spirit. Because He wants us to know the Spirit, He is showing us the river. When we see the Spirit of God as a great flowing river, we can better understand how to step into it and how to flow with its currents. The river is the Holy Spirit and the flow of the river is the outpouring of the Spirit. Whatever brings us to the river, if we can all get into it, every need will be supplied.

ISBN 1-884369-87-1 $13.00

GOLDEN GLORY

by Ruth Ward Heflin

What is Golden Glory?

God has never stopped performing signs and wonders for those who believe, and He never will. What we are seeing in the dawning days of the new millennium, however, is something altogether new and different. God is suddenly sending a visible glory, a golden glory, as gold dust or glory dust, upon His people.

This golden glory is appearing on Christians of every denominational background. It comes to us as we pray and as we worship, but it is also falling upon us as we go about our daily activities.

This golden glory is being manifested to those who seek it, and also to some who don't. It is a sovereign act of God to show His presence and His power in these last days. It is a wake-up call for the nations, a visible sign to the whole world, this rain of God's Golden Glory.

ISBN 1-58158-001-0 $13.00

UNIFYING GLORY

by Ruth Ward Heflin

What is Unifying Glory?

- *It is the touch of glory that brings a divine joining of brother to brother.*
- *It is a miraculous unity of the diverse members of the family of God.*
- *It is the answer to the prayer of Jesus: "That they all may be one."*

God is calling us to live in the cloud of His glory, in the smoke of His presence. He wants His people to be known as "The People of the Glory Cloud," not "The People Divided Into a Thousand Denominations."

ISBN 1-58158-006-1 $13.00

HARVEST GLORY

by
Ruth Ward Heflin

What is Harvest Glory?

> *We are called for this day and this hour. Born for it. Destined for it. The time of* Harvest Glory.
>
> *You and I are making ourselves available as threshing instruments to bring in the end-time harvest, the harvest of the world.*
>
> *Strengthened together in God, we shall bring all the harvest into the barn. Not one grain shall be lost. This is* Harvest Glory.

Hardback edition; 432 pages with 40 pages of photographs.

ISBN 1-884369-81-2 $25.00

Ask for it at your favorite bookstore or from:

Calvary Books
11352 Heflin Lane
Ashland, VA 23005
(804) 798-7756
www.revivalglory2.org

Jerusalem, Zion, Israel and the Nations

by
Ruth Ward Heflin

"God is returning the focus once again to Jerusalem. The place of beginnings is also the place of endings. And God's endings are always glorious.

"This overview is by no means definitive, but an unfolding of scriptures coming into prominence in these days. As Moses saw the Promised Land from Nebo, one sees the world from Jerusalem."

— Ruth Heflin

ISBN 1-884369-65-0 $13.00

Ask for it at your favorite bookstore or from:

Calvary Books
11352 Heflin Lane
Ashland, VA 23005
(804) 798-7756
www.revivalglory2.org

God of Miracles
Eighty Years of the Miraculous

by
Edith Ward Heflin

"My life has been very exciting because I was always looking forward to the next miracle, the next answer to prayer, the next thing Jesus would do for me. I expect I have lived twenty lifetimes within these eighty years. The God of all miracles has been so good and so very gracious to me."

— Edith Heflin

As you become witness to a life that has spanned the period from Azusa Street to this next great revival, the life of a unique woman who has known the great ministries of our century and has herself lived the life of the miraculous, you too will encounter the God of Miracles.

ISBN 1-56043-043-5 $10.00

Ask for it at your favorite bookstore or from:

Calvary Books
11352 Heflin Lane
Ashland, VA 23005
(804) 798-7756
www.revivalglory2.org

Hear the Voice of God

by
Wallace H. Heflin, Jr.

* Does God still speak to His people as He did to
  the prophets of old?
* If so, how does He speak?
* Can we actually hear His voice?
* What can we do to become more sensitive to
  God's voice?

Wallace Heflin, Jr., spent a lifetime hearing the voice of
God and following God's directives in dynamic ministry
to the people of this nation and the world. In this manuscript, the last one that he prepared before his death in
December of 1996, he challenges us that not only is it
possible to hear the voice of God, but that God actually
extends to every one of us an invitation to commune with
Him.

ISBN 1-884369-36-7 $12.00

Ask for it at your favorite bookstore or from:

Calvary Books
11352 Heflin Lane
Ashland, VA 23005
(804) 798-7756
www.revivalglory2.org

The Power of Prophecy

by
Wallace H. Heflin, Jr.

"Of all the nine gifts of the Spirit, prophecy is the gift that God is using most to bring in the revival of the end time. Because of that, it is prophecy that is being opposed now more than any other gift. I want to declare that it is time to take the limits off the gift of prophecy and off the prophets God has raised up for this hour. It is time to move into God's plan of action to declare His will prophetically to this, the final generation."

— Rev. Wallace Heflin, Jr.

- What is prophecy?
- What does it accomplish?
- Who can prophesy?
- How can YOU get started prophesying?

These and many other important questions are answered in this unique and timely volume.

ISBN 1-884369-22-7 $10.00

Ask for it at your favorite bookstore or from:

Calvary Books
11352 Heflin Lane
Ashland, VA 23005
(804) 798-7756
www.revivalglory2.org

Other books
by
Rev. Wallace H. Heflin, Jr.

A Pocket Full of Miracles	0-914903-23-3	$7.00
The Bride	1-884369-10-3	$7.00
Jacob and Esau	1-884369-01-4	$7.00
The Potter's House	1-884369-61-8	$9.00
Power in Your Hand	1-884369-60-X	$8.00

Power in Your Hand (Spanish Edition)
1-884369-04-9 $6.00

Ask for them at your favorite bookstore or from:

Calvary Books
11352 Heflin Lane
Ashland, VA 23005
(804) 798-7756
www.revivalglory2.org

Books by Dr. William A. Ward

Miracles That I Have Seen	1-884369-79-0	$13.00
God Can Turn Things Around	1-56043-014-1	$12.00
On the Edge of Time	0-91490347-0	$15.00
Get off the Ash Heap	1-884369-20-0	$9.00
Christian Cybernetics	1-884369-19-7	$10.00
How to Be Successful		$10.00

By Bob Shattles

Revival Fire and Glory	1-884369-84-7	$12.00
Souls Harvest	1-58158-003-7	$12.00

Ask for them at your favorite bookstore or from:

Calvary Books

11352 Heflin Lane
Ashland, VA 23005
(804) 798-7756
www.revivalglory2.org

Mount Zion Miracle Prayer Chapel

13 Ragheb Nashashibi
P.O. Box 20897
Sheikh Jarrah
Jerusalem, Israel

Tel. 972-2-5820902
Fax 972-2-5824725
www.revivalglory.org

Prayer Meetings:

2:00 – 3:00 P.M. Daily
Monday – Thursday

Services:
Friday, Saturday and Sunday
10:30 A.M.
7:30 P.M.
Pre-meeting praise 7:00 P.M.

Come and worship with us in Jerusalem!

Calvary Pentecostal Tabernacle

11352 Heflin Lane
Ashland, VA 23005

Tel. (804) 798-7756
Fax (804) 752-2163
www.revivalglory2.org

8 ½ Weeks of Summer Campmeeting 2001
Friday night, June 29 – Sunday night, August 26
With two great services daily, 11 A.M. & 8 P.M.

Winter Campmeeting 2002
February 1 – 24

Come and experience the glory with special speakers from around the world.

Revival Meetings
Each Friday night, Saturday morning, Saturday night and Sunday night in all other months

Ministry tapes and song tapes are also available upon request.